Collins

11+ Verbal Reasoning

Quick Practice Tests
Ages 10-11
Book 3

Giles Clare

Contents

About this book 3

Test 1	Move a Letter	4
Test 2	Code Pairs	5
Test 3	Complete the Sum	6
Test 4	Missing Three-letter Words	7
Test 5	Code Sets	8
Test 6	Word Analogies	9
Test 7	Letters for Numbers	10
Test 8	Related Words	11
Test 9	Complete the Third Pair the Same Way	12
Test 10	Hidden Words	13
Test 11	Letter Connections	14
Test 12	Letter Analogies	15
Test 13	Code Sequences	16
Test 14	Missing Three-letter Words	17
Test 15	Number Sequences	18
Test 16	Related Numbers	19
Test 17	Double Meanings	20
Test 18	Word Construction	21
Test 19	Synonyms	22
Test 20	Problem Solving	23
Test 21	Move a Letter	25
Test 22	Code Pairs	26
Test 23	Complete the Sum	27
Test 24	Missing Three-letter Words	28
Test 25	Code Sets	29
Test 26	Word Analogies	30
Test 27	Letters for Numbers	31
Test 28	Related Words	32
Test 29	Complete the Third Pair the Same Way	33
Test 30	Hidden Words	34
Test 31	Letter Connections	35
Test 32	Letter Analogies	36
Test 33	Code Sequences	37
Test 34	Missing Three-letter Words	38
Test 35	Number Sequences	39
Test 36	Related Numbers	40
Test 37	Double Meanings	41
Test 38	Word Combinations	42
Test 39	Synonyms	43
Test 40	Antonyms	44
Test 41	Move a Letter	45
Test 42	Code Pairs	46
Test 43	Complete the Sum	47
Test 44	Missing Three-letter Words	48
Test 45	Code Sets	49
Test 46	Word Analogies	50
Test 47	Letters for Numbers	51
Test 48	Related Words	52
Test 49	Complete the Third Pair the Same Way	53
Test 50	Hidden Words	54
Test 51	Letter Connections	55
Test 52	Letter Analogies	56
Test 53	Code Sequences	57
Test 54	Missing Three-letter Words	58
Test 55	Number Sequences	59
Test 56	Related Numbers	60
Test 57	Word Construction	61
Test 58	Word Combinations	62
Test 59	Antonyms	63
Test 60	Problem Solving	64
	Answers	67

About this book

Familiarisation with 11+ test-style questions is a critical step in preparing your child for the 11+ selection tests. This book gives children lots of opportunities to test themselves in short, manageable bursts, helping to build confidence and improve the chance of test success.

It contains 60 tests designed to develop key verbal reasoning skills.

- Each test is designed to be completed within a short amount of time. Frequent, short bursts of revision are found to be more productive than lengthier sessions.

- GL Assessment tests can be quite time-pressured so these practice tests will help your child become accustomed to this style of questioning.

- We recommend your child uses a pencil to complete the tests, so that they can rub out the answers and try again later.

- Your child will need a pencil and a rubber to complete the tests as well as some spare paper for rough working. They will also need to be able to see a clock/watch and should have a quiet place in which to do the tests.

- Your child should **not** use a calculator for any of these tests.

- Answers to each question are provided at the back of the book, with explanations given where appropriate.

- After completing the tests, your child should revisit their weaker areas and attempt to improve their scores and timings.

For more information about 11+ preparation and other practice resources available from Collins, go to our website at:

collins.co.uk/11plus

Test 1 — Move a Letter

You have 6 minutes to complete this test.
You have 10 questions to complete within the time given.

In each question, one letter can be moved from the first word to the second word to create two new words.

The order of the other letters must not change.

Underline the letter that needs to move, and write in the two new words.

EXAMPLE

fl<u>o</u>at   fund   _flat_   _found_

1. going   bass
2. house   moth
3. trace   plan
4. world   pace
5. shove   cure
6. table   road
7. chain   cost
8. ridge   clan
9. steep   size
10. swift   oven

Score: ………… / 10

Test 2: Code Pairs

You have 8 minutes to complete this test.
You have 10 questions to complete within the time given.

Use the alphabet below to help you with these questions.

A B C D E F G H I J K L M N O P Q R S T U V W X Y Z

In each question, use the code provided to identify the new word or code.

EXAMPLE

If the code for **LOST** is **JMQR**, what is the code for **FIND**?   DGLB

(each letter is −2)

1. If the code for **EXTRA** is **HUVPB**, what is the code for **ABOVE**?

2. If the code for **HEALTH** is **JHEQZO**, what is the code for **SCARCE**?

3. If the code for **PUPIL** is **OQRKF**, what word is created by the code **VAKIB**?

4. If the code for **UPLOAD** is **YKIWEF**, what word is created by the code **XMBUST**?

5. If the code for **NOTEBOOK** is **LQTKBTJN**, what word is created by the code **DNOARNNK**?

6. If the code for **FEARFUL** is **LUFRAEF**, what is the code for **SERIOUS**?

7. If the code for **CANOE** is **AWHGU**, what word is created by the code **EQCDJ**?

8. If the code for **COMPLAIN** is **JMIRFDHM**, what is the code for **PERCEIVE**?

9. If the code for **TRIUMPH** is **XPNBVUK**, what is the code for **OCEANIC**?

10. If the code for **DIVIDED** is **GEZAIOK**, what word is created by the code **QQGDJKY**?

Score: .... / 10

Test 3 — Complete the Sum

You have 6 minutes to complete this test.

You have 10 questions to complete within the time given.

In each question, write in the number that correctly completes the sum.

EXAMPLE

3 + 8 = __6__ + 5

1) 17 + 9 − 2 = ... × 6

2) (72 ÷ 6) + (16 ÷ 2) = 100 ÷ ....

3) 54 − 18 = 12 × ....

4) 9^2 + (3 × 3) = 10^2 − ....

5) 5 × 8 ÷ 2 + 6 = ... + (6 × 3)

6) (100 − 52) × 2 = 150 − ....

7) 55 ÷ 11 + 9 − 3 = 3^2 + ...

8) (9 × 8) − 4^2 = ... × 8

9) 12 × 11 + (4 × 7) = 185 − ....

10) 3 × 3 × 2 × 3 = 6 × ....

Score: .... / 10

Missing Three-letter Words

Test 4

You have 6 minutes to complete this test.

You have 10 questions to complete within the time given.

In each question, three letters have been removed from the word in capitals.

These three letters correctly spell a new word without changing their order.

Write in the three missing letters.

EXAMPLE

I used a COMER to do my homework project. ....**PUT**........

(*The word in capitals is COMPUTER.*)

1. My brother prefers peanuts to walnuts and CAWS. ....

2. There were no VACIES at the hotel that evening. ....

3. She showed her CAGE in the face of danger. ....

4. The two friends did everything TOHER. ....

5. I dropped the vase and it STERED on the floor. ....

6. Eloise CLED that Ava had taken her ruler. ....

7. A kind person handed in my WET to the police. ....

8. Henry REED his subscription to the gaming service. ....

9. Our cat won't stop clawing the FITURE. ....

10. The soldiers saluted when the COLL entered the room. ....

Score: .... / 10

1. WERE = 1343
2. 3425 = ERAS
3. SAVE = 5263
4. SORT = 3978
5. 4968 = MOLT
6. TRAM = 8724
7. GLOW = 2416
8. 3416 = SLOW
9. OWLS = 1643

Word Analogies

Test 6

You have 6 minutes to complete this test.
You have 10 questions to complete within the time given.

In each question, underline the two words (one from each group) that will complete the phrase in the best way.

EXAMPLE

Run is to
(<u>bolt</u> sword walk)
as **follow** is to
(watch leave <u>track</u>).   *(the words are synonyms)*

1. **Spade** is to
   (tool dig diamond)
   as **torch** is to
   (burn club illuminate).

2. **Foot** is to
   (length kick human)
   as **paw** is to
   (rodent scratch inch).

3. **Drive** is to
   (steer train golf)
   as **fly** is to
   (land hole plane).

4. **Kit** is to
   (ferret tick model)
   as **elver** is to
   (lever young eel).

5. **One** is to
   (two single won)
   as **eight** is to
   (ate seven double).

6. **Simple** is to
   (pretentious elementary complex)
   as **cross** is to
   (shape irate hybrid).

7. **Draw** is to
   (hospital paint ward)
   as **reward** is to
   (sketch nurse drawer).

8. **Always** is to
   (never soon today)
   as **seldom** is to
   (tomorrow often already).

9. **Television** is to
   (faraway show remote)
   as **computer** is to
   (monitor mouse proximity).

10. **Minute** is to
    (tiny time hour)
    as **witty** is to
    (clock second droll).

Score: .... / 10

Test 7 — Letters for Numbers

You have 6 minutes to complete this test.
You have 10 questions to complete within the time given.

In each question, numbers are shown as letters. Find the answer to the sum and write it in as a letter.

EXAMPLE

A = 3   B = 5   C = 24   D = 9   E = 25
What is the answer to this sum **written as a letter**?   A × B + D = ……C……   (3 × 5 + 9 = 24)

1) A = 12   B = 2   C = 11   D = 10   E = 6
What is the answer to this sum **written as a letter**?   E + (D ÷ B) = …………

2) A = 6   B = 28   C = 18   D = 21   E = 14
What is the answer to this sum **written as a letter**?   (E − A) + (E + A) = …………

3) A = 9   B = 10   C = 4   D = 3   E = 12
What is the answer to this sum **written as a letter**?   (C × A) ÷ D = …………

4) A = 1   B = 7   C = 2   D = 10   E = 3
What is the answer to this sum **written as a letter**?   B + B − D − E = …………

5) A = 4   B = 3   C = 1   D = 40   E = 17
What is the answer to this sum **written as a letter**?   (B + E) ÷ (C + A) = …………

6) A = 30   B = 7   C = 3   D = 27   E = 18
What is the answer to this sum **written as a letter**?   E ÷ C + (C × B) = …………

7) A = 25   B = 35   C = 40   D = 20   E = 10
What is the answer to this sum **written as a letter**?   A + (C − D − E) = …………

8) A = 1   B = 50   C = 2   D = 10   E = 0
What is the answer to this sum **written as a letter**?   (B ÷ D) − (D ÷ C) = …………

9) A = 66   B = 36   C = 30   D = 26   E = 16
What is the answer to this sum **written as a letter**?   (C + B + E) − E = …………

10) A = 11   B = 10   C = 33   D = 14   E = 12
What is the answer to this sum **written as a letter**?   (A × E) ÷ (D − B) = …………

Score: ………… / 10

Test 8: Related Words

You have 6 minutes to complete this test.
You have 10 questions to complete within the time given.

In each question, three of the words are related in some way.
Underline the two words that do not relate to the other three.

EXAMPLE

house   <u>theatre</u>   cottage   apartment   <u>cinema</u>

(all the others are places where people live)

1) hand   foot   yard   brick   stone

2) troop   pack   swarm   rush   soldier

3) hinder   raise   drop   boost   hoist

4) piece   dice   jigsaw   turn   console

5) biased   partial   light   unjust   festival

6) kite   helicopter   owl   crane   rhombus

7) licence   field   departure   passport   gate

8) bread   sugar   steak   yoghurt   cheese

9) ashamed   sheepish   selfish   contrite   proud

10) satisfied   share   content   message   distribute

Score: .... / 10

Test 9: Complete the Third Pair the Same Way

You have 6 minutes to complete this test.

You have 10 questions to complete within the time given.

Find the word that completes the third pair of words so that it follows the same pattern as the first two pairs.

EXAMPLE

wire wore   nine none   ship ...shop...

(change the 'i' to an 'o')

1. field yield   beast yeast   model ....
2. compact moat   balance lane   potatoes ....
3. cheers sheer   leap pea   rink ....
4. sand send   band bend   wall ....
5. doctor rot   minnow won   spare ....
6. medical dice   petunia tune   smite ....
7. dame came   nail mail   corn ....
8. stark start   formal format   wild ....
9. coppice cop   fitness sit   mandate ....
10. tow toe   throw throe   shows ....

Score: .... / 10

Test 10

Hidden Words

You have 6 minutes to complete this test.

You have 10 questions to complete within the time given.

In each question, a four-letter word can be found by combining the end (or whole) of one word with the beginning (or whole) of the next word.

Underline the two words that contain these letters and write in the new four-letter word.

EXAMPLE

I got some fresh air on my walk. ....hair....... (fresh air)

1. Sara was beaten by the quick newcomer in the race. ....

2. My pet rat escaped last night. ....

3. Someone had dropped their kebab leftovers on the floor. ....

4. The calypso melody danced through the balmy night. ....

5. She left the fruit pie resting on a windowsill. ....

6. Please tidy away all your art materials. ....

7. Anthrax is a rare disease spread by bacterial spores. ....

8. The fishermen uncovered a strange fossil by the cliff. ....

9. They found themselves in an eerie, ruined arena. ....

10. The citizens of the city persuaded the tyrant to leave. ....

Score: .... / 10

Test 11: Letter Connections

You have 6 minutes to complete this test.
You have 10 questions to complete within the time given.

In each question, write in the letter that fits into both sets of brackets.

The letter should finish the word before the brackets and start the word after the brackets.

EXAMPLE

dea [..f..] ont

hal [..f..] ew   (*The four words are deaf, font, half and few.*)

1. you [......] oad
   moo [......] aid

2. the [......] ob
   spa [......] ask

3. har [......] ray
   yel [......] age

4. plan [......] nit
   stea [......] in

5. her [......] live
   temp [......] pen

6. as [......] edge
   hig [......] ill

7. them [......] lite
   quit [......] very

8. ami [......] rier
   fun [......] raft

9. vi [......] tom
   coco [......] gain

10. blo [......] all
    chi [......] ould

Score: .... / 10

Test 12 — Letter Analogies

You have 6 minutes to complete this test.
You have 10 questions to complete within the time given.

Use the alphabet below to help you with these questions.

A B C D E F G H I J K L M N O P Q R S T U V W X Y Z

In each question, write the letters that will complete the phrase in the best way.

EXAMPLE

UC is to TG as NB is to ......MF......

(1st letter: –1; 2nd letter: +4)

1. FJ is to HN as TU is to ....

2. MK is to HC as SQ is to ....

3. PT is to SQ as XW is to ....

4. GC is to WA as OX is to ....

5. BW is to HF as RE is to ....

6. HA is to MZ as WL is to ....

7. CI is to NK as LF is to ....

8. VC is to PF as GX is to ....

9. TX is to PX as CJ is to ....

10. HI is to OP as EG is to ....

Score: .... / 10

Test 13 — Code Sequences

You have 6 minutes to complete this test.
You have 10 questions to complete within the time given.

Use the alphabet below to help you with these questions.

A B C D E F G H I J K L M N O P Q R S T U V W X Y Z

In each question, find the letters that are next in the sequence.

EXAMPLE

CK   FM   IJ   LN   OI   __RO__

(1st letter: +3; 2nd letter: +2, –3, +4, –5, +6)

1) TE   RH   PK   NN   LQ   ....

2) BZ   CV   ER   HN   LJ   ....

3) XD   XB   YX   YR   ZJ   ....

4) DG   WI   CJ   VL   BM   ....

5) VO   QD   MQ   JF   HS   ....

6) AM   CN   EP   GQ   IS   ....

7) EC   ZG   DK   YO   CS   ....

8) HH   EF   BD   YB   VZ   ....

9) GW   NP   JU   QN   MS   ....

10) YC   ZB   AA   BZ   CY   ....

Score: .... / 10

Test 14: Missing Three-letter Words

You have 6 minutes to complete this test.

You have 10 questions to complete within the time given.

In each question, three letters have been removed from the word in capitals.

These three letters correctly spell a new word without changing their order.

Write in the three missing letters.

EXAMPLE

We DEED the topic of using phones in school. .... BAT ....

(*The word in capitals is DE*BAT*ED.*)

1. A search revealed a SAWAY hiding in the ship's hold. ....

2. The police asked each EITNESS about the incident. ....

3. With the battle lost, the general ordered the RETR. ....

4. My dad tries to EMRASS me in front of my friends. ....

5. At the football match, everyone joined in with the ANT. ....

6. The cut on his leg developed into a KEROUS wound. ....

7. Yesterday, we ADED a cat from the shelter. ....

8. She always MISS her reading glasses at work. ....

9. The plastic toy had been DEMED by the intense heat. ....

10. My grandfather built a MAHOG chest of drawers. ....

Score: .... / 10

Test 15 — Number Sequences

You have 6 minutes to complete this test.

You have 10 questions to complete within the time given.

For each question, write in the number that completes the sequence.

EXAMPLE

51   49   47   45   43   ...... **41** ......   (the sequence is −2)

1)   6   20   34   48   62   ....

2)   729   243   81   27   9   ....

3)   6   8   12   20   36   ....

4)   81   64   49   36   25   ....

5)   25   20   30   15   35   ....

6)   13   13   12   10   7   ....

7)   2   3   7   11   13   ....

8)   15   30   60   120   240   ....

9)   2   3   5   8   13   ....

10)   75   64   53   42   31   ....

Score: .... / 10

Test 16 — Related Numbers

You have 6 minutes to complete this test.
You have 10 questions to complete within the time given.

In each question, the three numbers in each group are related in some way.
Write in the number that correctly completes the last group.

EXAMPLE

(5 [9] 13)   (23 [28] 33)   (12 [14] 16)

(The middle number is halfway between the outer two numbers.)

1. (42 [14] 56)   (35 [19] 54)   (23 [......] 60)

2. (5 [16] 8)   (12 [35] 20)   (8 [......] 12)

3. (9 [18] 3)   (11 [36] 5)   (2 [......] 4)

4. (2 [20] 9)   (5 [47] 21)   (9 [......] 10)

5. (16 [5] 4)   (18 [10] 2)   (30 [......] 3)

6. (2 [7] 6)   (4 [33] 2)   (3 [......] 3)

7. (10 [49] 3)   (11 [16] 7)   (12 [......] 9)

8. (4 [40] 5)   (7 [126] 9)   (10 [......] 11)

9. (2 [3] 12)   (1 [21] 24)   (3 [......] 15)

10. (10 [15] 5)   (22 [38] 6)   (11 [......] 8)

Score: .... / 10

Test 17: Double Meanings

You have 6 minutes to complete this test.
You have 10 questions to complete within the time given.

In each question, there are two pairs of words. Write in a new word that goes equally well with both word pairs.

EXAMPLE

(play   musical)
(exhibit   reveal)   ....show.......

1. (release   reduce)
   (bead   globule)   ....

2. (honourable   correct)
   (privilege   entitlement)   ....

3. (prevent   thwart)
   (station   halt)   ....

4. (fruit   leaf)
   (cluck   purr)   ....

5. (guide   command)
   (copper   aluminium)   ....

6. (vault   bound)
   (winter   summer)   ....

7. (flee   run)
   (fasten   secure)   ....

8. (fall   stumble)
   (journey   excursion)   ....

9. (whale   human)
   (tolerate   endure)   ....

10. (afflict   trouble)
    (pestilence   epidemic)   ....

Score: .... / 10

Test	**Word Construction**
18	You have 6 minutes to complete this test. You have 10 questions to complete within the time given. 

In each question, the three words on the second line should go together in the same way as the three words on the first line.

Write in the missing word on the second line.

EXAMPLE

(slap   [last]   this)

(skin   [.....**kind**.....]   down)

(word one letter 2, word one letter 3, word two letter 4, word two letter 1)

① (aunt   [dame]   dome)

 (earn   [..............]   lift)

② (herb   [home]   mood)

 (peak   [..............]   nice)

③ (zinc   [crib]   blur)

 (fret   [..............]   nano)

④ (dusk   [sulk]   flux)

 (gold   [..............]   heir)

⑤ (iris   [rink]   knee)

 (rage   [..............]   diet)

⑥ (lure   [lump]   poem)

 (redo   [..............]   data)

⑦ (tape   [peas]   bias)

 (both   [..............]   swan)

⑧ (soft   [gown]   wing)

 (road   [..............]   seen)

⑨ (foam   [made]   idle)

 (iron   [..............]   burn)

⑩ (scan   [calm]   limb)

 (drip   [..............]   oath)

Score: .... / 10

Test 19 — Synonyms

You have 6 minutes to complete this test.
You have 10 questions to complete within the time given.

In each question, underline the two words (one from each group) that are most similar in meaning.

EXAMPLE

(warning   bell   <u>alarm</u>)
(<u>startle</u>   ring   calm)

1. (sound   noise   racket)
   (silence   bat   loud)

2. (edge   face   garden)
   (border   grow   wash)

3. (danger   signal   rescue)
   (fetch   worry   indicate)

4. (tough   sharp   bend)
   (keen   blade   soft)

5. (time   see   watch)
   (strike   clock   hour)

6. (light   flame   spark)
   (simple   flimsy   night)

7. (clear   block   vague)
   (void   leave   obvious)

8. (hinder   agree   hold)
   (aid   accommodate   check)

9. (shout   total   partial)
   (utter   fair   reasonable)

10. (wrong   right   left)
    (straight   privilege   invert)

Score: .... / 10

Problem Solving

Test 20

You have 8 minutes to complete this test.

You have 8 questions to complete within the time given.

In each question, read the information provided and then write in your answer.

EXAMPLE

The classroom clock shows a time of 9:35 am.

The clock is running 6 minutes fast. Break is at 10:15 am.

How long is it in minutes until break starts?   ......46 minutes......

1. Mia, Aisha and Noah like apples.

   Liam and Cheng like bananas.

   Jasmine is the only one who doesn't like grapes.

   Aisha and Liam like oranges.

   All the boys and Mia like blueberries.

   Everyone apart from Noah likes mangoes.

   Aisha likes strawberries.

   How many more fruits does Aisha like than Jasmine? ....

2. Farah saw a pair of jeans online at Shop A that normally cost £25. The jeans are advertised as 25% off the normal price. The delivery charge is £5. She saw the same jeans online at Shop B for £29 with 50% off the price. The delivery charge is £9.

   How much cheaper are the jeans in Shop B than Shop A, including discounts and charges? ....

3. There are five paddling pools at a nursery.

   Pool A contains 400 litres of water.

   Pool B contains twice as much as Pool D.

   Pool E contains 350 litres but loses 12 litres a day because of a leak. At the end of a week, it contains 20 litres less than Pool B.

   Pool C contains 50 more litres than Pool A.

   How much more water is there in Pool C than Pool D? ....

Questions continue on next page

4 The time in 45 minutes will be 10:41 am.

What was the time 12 hours and 30 minutes ago? ....

5 The sum of two square numbers is 29.
The sum of two other square numbers is 113.

What is the total of the smallest and the largest square numbers used in the two sums above? ....

6 Colin is Stewart's uncle.
Violet is Evan's grandmother.
William is Violet's brother-in-law.
Stewart, Evan and Samuel are brothers.

What relation is William to Samuel? ....

7 In a race, Runner A is leading and then loses two places. Runner B is in 5th place and then gains one place. Runner C finishes the race in the top three. At the finish, the runner in 4th place overtakes the runner in 3rd place and finishes immediately behind Runner C.

In what position did Runner C finish? ....

8 Sanjay walks 200 m in a southerly direction. He then turns to his left. After walking 100 m, he turns to his right and walks 500 m. He then turns to his right again and stops to admire the view in front of him.

What direction is the view from his position? ....

Score: .... / 8

Test 21

Move a Letter

You have 6 minutes to complete this test.
You have 10 questions to complete within the time given.

In each question, one letter can be moved from the first word to the second word to create two new words.

The order of the other letters must not change.

Underline the letter that needs to move, and write in the two new words.

EXAMPLE

flo̲at   fund   ......flat......   ......found......

1. skill   than   ....
2. blame   ring   ....
3. point   avid   ....
4. began   race   ....
5. raise   long   ....
6. flies   rile   ....
7. sleep   east   ....
8. brand   heat   ....
9. every   prim   ....
10. debut   site   ....

Score: .... / 10

Test 22: Code Pairs

You have 8 minutes to complete this test.
You have 10 questions to complete within the time given.

Use the alphabet below to help you with these questions.

A B C D E F G H I J K L M N O P Q R S T U V W X Y Z

In each question, use the code provided to identify the new word or code.

EXAMPLE

If the code for **LOST** is **JMQR**, what is the code for **FIND**?   DGLB

(each letter is −2)

1. If the code for **DICE** is **FJEF**, what is the code for **HOST**?

2. If the code for **EARLY** is **DXMEP**, what is the code for **ELBOW**?

3. If the code for **FAMILY** is **FBMKLB**, what word is created by the code **PVRUUH**?

4. If the code for **SENIOR** is **YZRFQQ**, what is the code for **FLORAL**?

5. If the code for **COLD** is **FPNE**, what word is created by the code **NFTC**?

6. If the code for **AGENT** is **KLNRB**, what is the code for **BRUSH**?

7. If the code for **HUNDRED** is **JWPFTGF**, what word is created by the code **MKPIFQO**?

8. If the code for **JAUNT** is **EDNQN**, what word is created by the code **NPBOY**?

9. If the code for **BELONG** is **GNOLEB**, what is the code for **RELIEF**?

10. If the code for **EXACT** is **DZXGO**, what word is created by the code **VCIXU**?

Score: .... / 10

Complete the Sum

Test 23

You have 6 minutes to complete this test.

You have 10 questions to complete within the time given.

In each question, write in the number that correctly completes the sum.

EXAMPLE

$3 + 8 = \underline{6} + 5$

1. $14 \times 2 - 10 = 2 \times \underline{}$

2. $9 + 4 + (4 \times 6) = \underline{} + 5^2$

3. $(3^2 + 2^2) \times 2 = \underline{} - 14$

4. $3 \times (8 \div 4) + 8^2 = 9 + \underline{}$

5. $99 \div 3 + 9 = \underline{} \times 6$

6. $(84 \div 3) \div 4 = 63 \div \underline{}$

7. $(16 \div 2) + (50 \times 3) = 212 - \underline{}$

8. $7 \times 8 + (7 \times 6) = \underline{} - 100$

9. $4^3 \times 2 = \underline{}^2 \times 2$

10. $3^3 - (3 + 15) = 36 \div \underline{}$

Score: .... / 10

Test 24: Missing Three-letter Words

You have 6 minutes to complete this test.

You have 10 questions to complete within the time given.

In each question, three letters have been removed from the word in capitals.

These three letters correctly spell a new word without changing their order.

Write in the three missing letters.

EXAMPLE

I used a COMER to do my homework project. ......**PUT**......

(*The word in capitals is COMPUTER.*)

1. The treasure chest opened, RALING a hoard of coins and jewels. ....

2. Last summer, the weather was BING for ten days in a row. ....

3. The SLTHY cat crept silently across the rooftops. ....

4. I forgot to pack spare TRORS for my trip abroad. ....

5. The cyclist swerved and NARRY avoided the pothole. ....

6. Drama club meets to REHSE every Tuesday lunchtime. ....

7. Many everyday items are CHER in the new shop. ....

8. FNSIC analysis of the evidence led to an arrest. ....

9. Crude oil from the REERY spilled into a river. ....

10. I had no idea he was the VAIN until the twist at the end. ....

Score: .... / 10

Test 25 — Code Sets

You have 6 minutes to complete this test.

You have 9 questions to complete within the time given (3 sets of codes with 3 questions each).

In each set of questions, three of the four words are given in code. These codes are not in the same order as the words and one code is missing. Use these codes to answer each question and write your answer on the dotted line.

EXAMPLE

PALM	REAL	SURE	PLAN
2163	4639	4365	

Find the code for the word **PALM**. ......4639......

STEP	PEST	STOP	POSE
2461	1524	2451	

(1) Find the code for the word **PEST**. ....

(2) Find the word for the code **2461**. ....

(3) Find the code for the word **POSE**. ....

FIRE	LIFE	LEND	FIND
7253	7240	6053	

(4) Find the code for the word **LEND**. ....

(5) Find the word for the code **7253**. ....

(6) Find the code for the word **LIFE**. ....

HOUR	HURT	RUSH	TOUR
5314	4162	2314	

(7) Find the code for the word **TOUR**. ....

(8) Find the word for the code **4162**. ....

(9) Find the code for the word **HURT**. ....

Score: .... / 9

Word Analogies

Test 26

You have 6 minutes to complete this test.
You have 10 questions to complete within the time given.

In each question, underline the two words (one from each group) that will complete the phrase in the best way.

EXAMPLE

Run is to
(<u>bolt</u> sword walk)
as **follow** is to
(watch leave <u>track</u>).   *(the words are synonyms)*

1. **Berry** is to
   (fruit blue bury)
   as **right** is to
   (wrong write healthy).

2. **Throw** is to
   (pull cast each)
   as **snare** is to
   (drum drop catch).

3. **Sail** is to
   (yacht motor cruise)
   as **paddle** is to
   (canoe swim water).

4. **Fast** is to
   (hilly slowly gully)
   as **hard** is to
   (bully softly wobbly).

5. **Airport** is to
   (armpit pencil monkey)
   as **scarecrow** is to
   (chimney mountain passport).

6. **Keyboard** is to
   (mouse letter type)
   as **ruler** is to
   (measure tape monarch).

7. **Maps** is to
   (chart spam navigate)
   as **time** is to
   (space clock emit).

8. **Shoe** is to
   (foot sock chase)
   as **tie** is to
   (wrap neck draw).

9. **Hole** is to
   (poll punch ice)
   as **seal** is to
   (glue walrus pouch).

10. **Elephant** is to
    (tiger cow mammal)
    as **pig** is to
    (insect sheep sow).

Score: .... / 10

Test 27: Letters for Numbers

You have 6 minutes to complete this test.
You have 10 questions to complete within the time given.

In each question, numbers are shown as letters. Find the answer to the sum and write it in as a letter.

EXAMPLE

A = 3 B = 5 C = 24 D = 9 E = 25
What is the answer to this sum **written as a letter**?   A × B + D = __C__   (3 × 5 + 9 = 24)

1) A = 30   B = 2   C = 10   D = 15   E = 3
What is the answer to this sum **written as a letter**?   D × B ÷ E = ...

2) A = 1   B = 67   C = 5   D = 11   E = 27
What is the answer to this sum **written as a letter**?   (D + A) + (D × C) = ...

3) A = 20   B = 16   C = 26   D = 56   E = 46
What is the answer to this sum **written as a letter**?   C + (C + A − B) = ...

4) A = 49   B = 12   C = 1   D = 6   E = 84
What is the answer to this sum **written as a letter**?   (E ÷ B) × (B ÷ C) = ...

5) A = 48   B = 5   C = 15   D = 3   E = 40
What is the answer to this sum **written as a letter**?   B × (A ÷ D) − E = ...

6) A = 19   B = 18   C = 27   D = 31   E = 21
What is the answer to this sum **written as a letter**?   D − (E + B − C) = ...

7) A = 9   B = 32   C = 24   D = 8   E = 3
What is the answer to this sum **written as a letter**?   A × D ÷ E + D = ...

8) A = 13   B = 5   C = 15   D = 12   E = 10
What is the answer to this sum **written as a letter**?   (B × B × B − B) ÷ E = ...

9) A = 69   B = 2   C = 29   D = 99   E = 9
What is the answer to this sum **written as a letter**?   (C × B) + (D ÷ E) = ...

10) A = 107   B = 11   C = 18   D = 80   E = 78
What is the answer to this sum **written as a letter**?   A − B − C = ...

Score: .... / 10

Test 28 — Related Words

You have 6 minutes to complete this test.
You have 10 questions to complete within the time given.

In each question, three of the words are related in some way.
Underline the two words that do not relate to the other three.

EXAMPLE

house   <u>theatre</u>   cottage   apartment   <u>cinema</u>

(all the others are places where people live)

1. stern   axle   bow   wing   deck
2. hamper   table   picnic   prevent   impede
3. goat   kid   jest   tease   adult
4. rotator   kayak   river   madam   professor
5. ancient   rattle   tap   modern   ballet
6. engine   steam   desert   ice   water
7. deer   sheep   hamster   wolf   moose
8. emit   omit   neglect   overlook   watch
9. turn   courage   mind   lack   sign
10. town   village   continent   city   region

Score: .... / 10

Test 29: Complete the Third Pair the Same Way

You have 6 minutes to complete this test.

You have 10 questions to complete within the time given.

Find the word that completes the third pair of words so that it follows the same pattern as the first two pairs.

EXAMPLE

wire wore nine none ship ......**shop**......

(change the 'i' to an 'o')

1) part trap flow wolf rail ....

2) scared scored farmer former warship ....

3) tingle single hector sector revere ....

4) giant gain gaols goal deity ....

5) lord laud tort taut gorge ....

6) coast coats pried pride angel ....

7) formal farm fallen fell fondue ....

8) trace crate leaps peals serve ....

9) venture rent dollar roll tensile ....

10) crow crux theme thine chart ....

Score: .... / 10

Hidden Words

Test 30

You have **6 minutes** to complete this test.

You have **10 questions** to complete within the time given.

In each question, a four-letter word can be found by combining the end (or whole) of one word with the beginning (or whole) of the next word.

Underline the two words that contain these letters and write in the new four-letter word.

EXAMPLE

I got some fre<u>sh air</u> on my walk. ……… *hair* ……… (fre**sh** **air**)

1) Mum ordered a huge sushi platter as a treat. ……………

2) Our hardware provides a total solution for your business. ……………

3) Enjoy the stunning natural wonders of the Lake District this year. ……………

4) My aunt and uncle both studied geography at university. ……………

5) After the science fair, I took my prize-winning robot home. ……………

6) There is a lorry stuck going westbound on the dual carriageway. ……………

7) A hovercraft is a complex amphibious vehicle. ……………

8) Yesterday, I broke my tibia slipping on a wet floor. ……………

9) The council voted to allow new independent shops on the high street. ……………

10) My grandfather always takes a thick notepad on walks for sketching. ……………

Score: ……… / 10

Letter Connections

Test 31

You have 6 minutes to complete this test.

You have 10 questions to complete within the time given.

In each question, write in the letter that fits into both sets of brackets.

The letter should finish the word before the brackets and start the word after the brackets.

EXAMPLE

dea [...f...] ont

hal [...f...] ew   (*The four words are deaf, font, half and few.*)

1. blur [............] id
   plum [............] red

2. rene [............] on
   bro [............] hen

3. leas [............] dit
   hug [............] ager

4. opu [............] lot
   alia [............] how

5. wai [............] lung
   cle [............] lora

6. stun [............] ash
   ran [............] low

7. sar [............] deal
   umam [............] ota

8. rena [............] it
   bow [............] each

9. have [............] ous
   logi [............] ode

10. fee [............] sar
    meri [............] own

Score: .... / 10

Test 32 — Letter Analogies

You have 6 minutes to complete this test.
You have 10 questions to complete within the time given.

Use the alphabet below to help you with these questions.

A B C D E F G H I J K L M N O P Q R S T U V W X Y Z

In each question, write the letters that will complete the phrase in the best way.

EXAMPLE

UC is to TG as NB is to ....MF........

(1st letter: −1; 2nd letter: +4)

1. DL is to FO as NR is to ....

2. ZM is to AH as GX is to ....

3. NE is to LD as QS is to ....

4. FF is to BJ as RR is to ....

5. XC is to FA as OG is to ....

6. BT is to YZ as DE is to ....

7. VH is to QD as LW is to ....

8. IV is to CE as ZH is to ....

9. AA is to DA as ZZ is to ....

10. LR is to MH as RL is to ....

Score: .... / 10

Code Sequences

Test 33

You have 6 minutes to complete this test.
You have 10 questions to complete within the time given.

Use the alphabet below to help you with these questions.

A B C D E F G H I J K L M N O P Q R S T U V W X Y Z

In each question, find the letters that are next in the sequence.

EXAMPLE

| CK | FM | IJ | LN | OI | RO |

(1st letter: +3; 2nd letter: +2, –3, +4, –5, +6)

1	AX	CU	FR	JO	OL	....
2	SZ	WX	AV	ET	IR	....
3	EM	NK	FH	OF	GC	....
4	VC	UC	SE	PE	LG	....
5	BW	AZ	ZC	YF	XI	....
6	FY	BT	XP	TM	PK	....
7	RD	UF	VH	YJ	ZL	....
8	PL	QD	SK	TC	VJ	....
9	CA	PZ	EY	RX	GW	....
10	CZ	DY	GV	LQ	SJ	....

Score: .... / 10

Test 34: Missing Three-letter Words

You have 6 minutes to complete this test.

You have 10 questions to complete within the time given.

In each question, three letters have been removed from the word in capitals.

These three letters correctly spell a new word without changing their order.

Write in the three missing letters.

EXAMPLE

We DEED the topic of using phones in school. ......**BAT**......

(The word in capitals is DE<u>BAT</u>ED.)

1. The engine in my vintage car keeps MISING and belching out smoke. ....

2. Early dinosaurs were scaly whereas some later ones were FEATED. ....

3. The film star received a large PAT in court from the newspaper. ....

4. My aunt slipped on some SEED and fell in a rock pool. ....

5. Molly needed to PURCE a new laptop for her business. ....

6. Dogs have a much more AE sense of smell than humans. ....

7. The cyclists were all struggling with the steep GRANT of the hill. ....

8. Beans, peas and lentils are LEES, a type of vegetable. ....

9. My doctor gave me a HYERMIC injection to help my injured shoulder. ....

10. The PLES on the beach had been shaped and smoothed by the waves. ....

Score: .... / 10

Number Sequences

Test 35

You have 6 minutes to complete this test.

You have 10 questions to complete within the time given.

For each question, write in the number that completes the sequence.

EXAMPLE

51   49   47   45   43   __41__   (the sequence is −2)

1) 55   46   37   28   19   ....

2) 1   3   9   27   81   ....

3) 14   15   18   23   30   ....

4) 216   125   64   27   8   ....

5) 192   96   48   24   12   ....

6) 11   9   9   11   7   ....

7) 1   2   2   4   8   ....

8) 20   25   30   20   40   ....

9) 99   101   105   111   119   ....

10) 29   23   19   17   13   ....

Score: .... / 10

Test 36: Related Numbers

You have 6 minutes to complete this test.
You have 10 questions to complete within the time given.

In each question, the three numbers in each group are related in some way.
Write in the number that correctly completes the last group.

EXAMPLE

(5 [9] 13)   (23 [28] 33)   (12 [__14__] 16)

(The middle number is halfway between the outer two numbers.)

1. (4 [6] 24)   (5 [8] 40)   (3 [......] 21)

2. (14 [32] 18)   (17 [30] 13)   (16 [......] 12)

3. (5 [10] 15)   (8 [54] 10)   (6 [......] 20)

4. (80 [40] 100)   (15 [70] 50)   (25 [......] 75)

5. (1 [28] 3)   (5 [13] 2)   (2 [......] 4)

6. (26 [8] 10)   (24 [5] 14)   (28 [......] 16)

7. (7 [51] 8)   (5 [45] 10)   (6 [......] 9)

8. (9 [86] 3)   (10 [112] 10)   (7 [......] 1)

9. (3 [33] 15)   (9 [31] 11)   (8 [......] 12)

10. (2 [18] 3)   (5 [90] 6)   (1 [......] 4)

Score: .... / 10

40

Double Meanings

Test 37

You have 6 minutes to complete this test.
You have 10 questions to complete within the time given.

In each question, there are two pairs of words. Write in a new word that goes equally well with both word pairs.

EXAMPLE

(play   musical)
(exhibit   reveal)   ....**show**....

1. (observe   view)
   (sundial   clock)   ....

2. (brand   marque)
   (assemble   build)   ....

3. (speech   lecture)
   (whereabouts   location)   ....

4. (flat   level)
   (inundate   wash)   ....

5. (mistaken   incorrect)
   (injustice   violation)   ....

6. (cause   encourage)
   (exactly   sharp)   ....

7. (rapid   speedy)
   (articulate   convey)   ....

8. (empty   unblock)
   (obvious   evident)   ....

9. (slide   glide)
   (flounder   plaice)   ....

10. (absolute   total)
    (conclude   finish)   ....

Score: .... / 10

Word Combinations

Test 38

You have 6 minutes to complete this test.
You have 10 questions to complete within the time given.

In each question, combine one word from the first group with one word from the second group to create one new word.

The word from the first group always comes first.

Underline the correct word from each group and write in the new word.

EXAMPLE

(<u>tooth</u> bed ache)
(skin sun <u>pick</u>)   toothpick

1. (earth air clean)
   (tight water plain) ....

2. (quick slow gold)
   (rapid silver ring) ....

3. (stop map flow)
   (atlas go chart) ....

4. (proof write strong)
   (wrong evidence read) ....

5. (steal through under)
   (sleep take over) ....

6. (sword knight long)
   (tunic hood robe) ....

7. (year worm annual)
   (meeting book cancel) ....

8. (lead singer loud)
   (speaker noise actor) ....

9. (club jump card)
   (bored spade suit) ....

10. (mend grip break)
    (hold hand fast) ....

Score: .... / 10

Test 39 — Synonyms

You have 6 minutes to complete this test.
You have 10 questions to complete within the time given.

In each question, underline the two words (one from each group) that are most similar in meaning.

EXAMPLE

(warning   bell   <u>alarm</u>)
(<u>startle</u>   ring   calm)

1. (yak   shake   cattle)
   (bull   prattle   milk)

2. (text   book   pamphlet)
   (scribe   reserve   reading)

3. (file   line   smooth)
   (rough   secret   folder)

4. (spoon   hat   field)
   (present   pitch   mud)

5. (accord   row   snow)
   (argument   bow   funnel)

6. (galaxy   press   star)
   (planet   gossip   celebrity)

7. (twist   howl   straight)
   (draught   path   wind)

8. (home   listen   address)
   (lecture   stay   hotel)

9. (sour   dessert   sandy)
   (arid   cactus   sweet)

10. (clip   raisin   desiccate)
    (water   prune   extend)

Score: .... / 10

Test 40 — Antonyms

You have 6 minutes to complete this test.
You have 10 questions to complete within the time given.

In each question, underline the two words (one from each group) that are most opposite in meaning.

EXAMPLE

(acidic <u>sharp</u> keen)
(crisp clever <u>blunt</u>)

1. (open warm close)
   (complete far near)

2. (tense charity future)
   (gift tight past)

3. (grave secular bury)
   (lay trivial stone)

4. (condition chopped mint)
   (damaged basil herb)

5. (game reject bank)
   (jilt loan grant)

6. (rest foundation excessive)
   (stand toil easy)

7. (solve calculated likely)
   (determine computed unplanned)

8. (disease harmful vaccinate)
   (illness innocuous attack)

9. (hunch svelte bend)
   (lean inkling proof)

10. (tomorrow year today)
    (annual yesterday week)

Score: .... / 10

Move a Letter

Test 41

You have 6 minutes to complete this test.
You have 10 questions to complete within the time given.

In each question, one letter can be moved from the first word to the second word to create two new words.

The order of the other letters must not change.

Underline the letter that needs to move, and write in the two new words.

EXAMPLE

fl<u>o</u>at   fund   ....flat.......   ....found.......

1) month   doze   ....

2) tired   crow   ....

3) crash   over   ....

4) moral   real   ....

5) flank   thin   ....

6) brain   mage   ....

7) carve   seen   ....

8) probe   clam   ....

9) rebel   fire   ....

10) lather   sock   ....

Score: .... / 10

45

Code Pairs

Test 42

You have 8 minutes to complete this test.

You have 10 questions to complete within the time given.

Use the alphabet below to help you with these questions.

A B C D E F G H I J K L M N O P Q R S T U V W X Y Z

In each question, use the code provided to identify the new word or code.

EXAMPLE

If the code for **LOST** is **JMQR**, what is the code for **FIND**?   DGLB

(each letter is –2)

1. If the code for **MYTH** is **NAWL**, what is the code for **CHIN**?

2. If the code for **ORGAN** is **NREAM**, what word is created by the code **HMNLX**?

3. If the code for **DIVERSE** is **ESREVID**, what word is created by the code **EDARGPU**?

4. If the code for **QUIT** is **STJR**, what is the code for **JOKE**?

5. If the code for **ENOUGH** is **BJLQDD**, what is the code for **FACTOR**?

6. If the code for **MOTHER** is **RTXLHU**, what word is created by the code **WJEWRQ**?

7. If the code for **ZEAL** is **ACDH**, what word is created by the code **PLBT**?

8. If the code for **FRESH** is **MUJTQ**, what is the code for **BEGIN**?

9. If the code for **CHARITY** is **EKCUKWA**, what word is created by the code **UWQPCFJ**?

10. If the code for **GRAB** is **ENLV**, what is the code for **KELP**?

Score: .... / 10

Complete the Sum

Test 43

You have 6 minutes to complete this test.

You have 10 questions to complete within the time given.

In each question, write in the number that correctly completes the sum.

EXAMPLE

3 + 8 = __6__ + 5

1) 8 × 9 = 7 × 6 + ...

2) 4^3 × 2 = 12^2 − ....

3) (96 − 8) ÷ 11 = ... ÷ 7

4) 5 × 6 × 2 = 20 + (.................. × 4)

5) 108 ÷ 3^2 = 2 × .... × 3

6) (17 − 3) + (21 − 7) = 19 + ...

7) 4 × (1 + 11) = 16 × ....

8) (3^2 + 2^3) − 7 = ... ÷ 5

9) 200 − (5 × 15) = 100 + ...^{2}

10) 11 × 6 = (32 + 54) − ....

Score: .... / 10

Missing Three-letter Words

Test 44

You have 6 minutes to complete this test.

You have 10 questions to complete within the time given.

In each question, three letters have been removed from the word in capitals.

These three letters correctly spell a new word without changing their order.

Write in the three missing letters.

EXAMPLE

I used a COMER to do my homework project. ......**PUT**......

(The word in capitals is COM*PUT*ER.)

1. He hopes to LATE his parents' success in business. ....

2. In the tall BEL, the church bells rang loudly. ....

3. Our GLLING adventure in the jungle was over at last. ....

4. Her natural athletic PRSS has been obvious since she was young. ....

5. They decided to DETE from the planned route. ....

6. It has been wonderful BANG by the pool all day. ....

7. The police MISK a passerby for the burglar. ....

8. A PESIDE can protect crops from insects. ....

9. The documentary was full of legal GON that made it hard to follow. ....

10. The students were put in new PINGS for the activity. ....

Score: .... / 10

Code Sets

Test 45

You have 6 minutes to complete this test.

You have 9 questions to complete within the time given (3 sets of codes with 3 questions each).

In each set of questions, three of the four words are given in code. These codes are not in the same order as the words and one code is missing. Use these codes to answer each question and write your answer on the dotted line.

EXAMPLE

PALM	REAL	SURE	PLAN
2163	4639	4365	

Find the code for the word **PALM**. ......4639......

REAM	LIED	IDLE	RIDE
2584	2417	5894	

1. Find the code for the word **RIDE**. ....

2. Find the word for the code **5894**. ....

3. Find the code for the word **LIED**. ....

TOME	COME	BEST	COST
4972	1268	4968	

4. Find the code for the word **BEST**. ....

5. Find the word for the code **4972**. ....

6. Find the code for the word **TOME**. ....

HYMN	THAN	MANY	MYTH
2943	3925	4375	

7. Find the code for the word **MYTH**. ....

8. Find the word for the code **4375**. ....

9. Find the code for the word **MANY**. ....

Score: .... / 9

Test 46: Word Analogies

You have 6 minutes to complete this test.
You have 10 questions to complete within the time given.

In each question, underline the two words (one from each group) that will complete the phrase in the best way.

EXAMPLE

Run is to (bolt sword walk) as **follow** is to (watch leave track). (*the words are synonyms*)

1. **Evil** is to (dead good live) as **stun** is to (hit surprise nuts).

2. **Cylinder** is to (cube octagon square) as **cone** is to (triangle tetrahedron circle).

3. **Menacing** is to (inviting baleful yard) as **serious** is to (grave stony comic).

4. **Right** is to (correct wrong east) as **left** is to (hand west direction).

5. **Pliable** is to (material plaster rigid) as **astute** is to (obtuse acute monument).

6. **Angel** is to (glean slang wings) as **players** is to (game layered parsley).

7. **Car** is to (fuel start key) as **window** is to (glass latch frame).

8. **Hinge** is to (elbow hip handle) as **pivot** is to (pilot saddle neck).

9. **Jupiter** is to (Pluto Zeus Mercury) as **Neptune** is to (Poseidon Hera Apollo).

10. **Mercy** is to (salt rainbow justice) as **hope** is to (leg courage noise).

Score: .... / 10

Test 47 — Letters for Numbers

You have 6 minutes to complete this test.
You have 10 questions to complete within the time given.

In each question, numbers are shown as letters. Find the answer to the sum and write it in as a letter.

EXAMPLE

A = 3   B = 5   C = 24   D = 9   E = 25
What is the answer to this sum **written as a letter**?   A × B + D = __C__   (3 × 5 + 9 = 24)

1. A = 12   B = 6   C = 4   D = 9   E = 1
What is the answer to this sum **written as a letter**?   A ÷ (E + E) = ...

2. A = 25   B = 4   C = 3   D = 2   E = 35
What is the answer to this sum **written as a letter**?   (B + C) × (D + C) = ...

3. A = 45   B = 56   C = 37   D = 7   E = 42
What is the answer to this sum **written as a letter**?   C + (B ÷ D) = ...

4. A = 6   B = 28   C = 24   D = 12   E = 8
What is the answer to this sum **written as a letter**?   (A × E) ÷ (E − A) = ...

5. A = 47   B = 1   C = 25   D = 11   E = 21
What is the answer to this sum **written as a letter**?   (A − C − E) × B = ...

6. A = 2   B = 4   C = 9   D = 45   E = 3
What is the answer to this sum **written as a letter**?   D ÷ E − (B + C) = ...

7. A = 12   B = 18   C = 3   D = 27   E = 4
What is the answer to this sum **written as a letter**?   (A × C × C) ÷ E = ...

8. A = 13   B = 24   C = 34   D = 29   E = 11
What is the answer to this sum **written as a letter**?   D + D − E − A = ...

9. A = 900   B = 10   C = 100   D = 90   E = 9
What is the answer to this sum **written as a letter**?   (B × E × B) ÷ C = ...

10. A = 80   B = 4   C = 50   D = 90   E = 60
What is the answer to this sum **written as a letter**?   (D − E) + (A ÷ B) = ...

Score: .... / 10

Related Words

Test 48

You have 6 minutes to complete this test.
You have 10 questions to complete within the time given.

In each question, three of the words are related in some way.
Underline the two words that do not relate to the other three.

EXAMPLE

house   <u>theatre</u>   cottage   apartment   <u>cinema</u>

(all the others are places where people live)

1) bee   ant   crawl   fly   centipede

2) bat   bowl   toast   evening   jam

3) seize   knees   weather   foreign   please

4) groom   dentist   analyst   farrier   farmer

5) err   correct   botch   fix   blunder

6) noon   moon   year   dusk   sunrise

7) turtle   tortoise   whale   seal   crab

8) bury   meet   join   serial   coffin

9) frost   cover   rail   trust   crease

10) cooking   poster   spray   oil   brush

Score: .... / 10

Test 49: Complete the Third Pair the Same Way

You have 6 minutes to complete this test.
You have 10 questions to complete within the time given.

Find the word that completes the third pair of words so that it follows the same pattern as the first two pairs.

EXAMPLE

wire wore   nine none   ship ....**shop**........

(change the 'i' to an 'o')

1. hand had   ploy ply   burn ....

2. sure sire   bull bill   foul ....

3. enact can   veils lie   start ....

4. durable blue   crushed herd   painter ....

5. overlap love   identify tide   avenger ....

6. sold solo   tempt tempo   crypts ....

7. teach torch   steak stork   weald ....

8. precious user   credible leer   hospital ....

9. straw warts   stink knits   sleep ....

10. hour ours   maim aims   bear ....

Score: .... / 10

Hidden Words

Test 50

You have 6 minutes to complete this test.

You have 10 questions to complete within the time given.

In each question, a four-letter word can be found by combining the end (or whole) of one word with the beginning (or whole) of the next word.

Underline the two words that contain these letters and write in the new four-letter word.

EXAMPLE

I got some fresh air on my walk.   hair   (*fresh air*)

1. Jamal was waiting <u>for</u> <u>t</u>he bus in the rain.   **fort**

2. Those yachts in that marin<u>a</u> <u>rea</u>lly impressed me.   **area**

3. His fir<u>st</u> <u>op</u>ponent was much stronger but not as quick.   **stop**

4. The cat has bit<u>ten</u> <u>t</u>he dog next door again.   **tent**

5. Archaeologists have discovered a fragi<u>le</u> <u>an</u>d precious crown.   **lean**

6. We hope for better weathe<u>r</u> <u>aft</u>er all this wind and snow.   **raft**

7. She was annoyed when her qui<u>che</u> <u>f</u>ell on the floor.   **chef**

8. He listens to mus<u>ic</u> <u>on</u>line, but he prefers vinyl records.   **icon**

9. You should in<u>put</u> <u>t</u>hat new data into the spreadsheet.   **putt**

10. Eliza took the old pony for a t<u>rot</u> <u>a</u>long the path.   **rota**

Score: .... / 10

Test 51: Letter Connections

You have 6 minutes to complete this test.
You have 10 questions to complete within the time given.

In each question, write in the letter that fits into both sets of brackets.

The letter should finish the word before the brackets and start the word after the brackets.

EXAMPLE

dea [f] ont

hal [f] ew   (The four words are deaf, font, half and few.)

1. men [......] nit
   haik [......] pend

2. glit [......] one
   topa [......] ero

3. are [......] ide
   sag [......] head

4. full [......] ours
   fort [......] east

5. poly [......] ie
   car [......] ace

6. loc [......] over
   pit [......] aunt

7. tal [......] at
   lila [......] oup

8. spor [......] bony
   win [......] pic

9. boa [......] uddy
   dete [......] adar

10. ago [......] rub
    blo [......] room

Score: .... / 10

Letter Analogies

Test 52

You have 6 minutes to complete this test.
You have 10 questions to complete within the time given.

Use the alphabet below to help you with these questions.

A B C D E F G H I J K L M N O P Q R S T U V W X Y Z

In each question, write the letters that will complete the phrase in the best way.

EXAMPLE

UC is to **TG** as **NB** is to ......**MF**......

(1st letter: −1; 2nd letter: +4)

1. **CF** is to **FH** as **QM** is to ....

2. **MV** is to **ER** as **FR** is to ....

3. **BX** is to **GS** as **IH** is to ....

4. **WZ** is to **AO** as **EW** is to ....

5. **KG** is to **DK** as **GX** is to ....

6. **TA** is to **YF** as **BD** is to ....

7. **QP** is to **HJ** as **LL** is to ....

8. **OU** is to **RR** as **GM** is to ....

9. **YL** is to **YV** as **EX** is to ....

10. **SE** is to **BN** as **FB** is to ....

Score: .... / 10

Code Sequences

Test 53

You have 6 minutes to complete this test.
You have 10 questions to complete within the time given.

Use the alphabet below to help you with these questions.

A B C D E F G H I J K L M N O P Q R S T U V W X Y Z

In each question, find the letters that are next in the sequence.

EXAMPLE

| CK | FM | IJ | LN | OI | RO |

(1st letter: +3; 2nd letter: +2, –3, +4, –5, +6)

1) BM DN FO HP JQ   ....

2) WA UF TK RP QU   ....

3) TW TT UQ WN ZK   ....

4) KR GS CQ YT UP   ....

5) AY TV BQ UN CI   ....

6) MJ QE OH SC QF   ....

7) NM HS BY VE PK   ....

8) GP WR JV ZB MJ   ....

9) HW GZ EC BF XI   ....

10) AB BX EW JS QR   ....

Score: .... / 10

Missing Three-letter Words

Test 54

You have 6 minutes to complete this test.

You have 10 questions to complete within the time given.

In each question, three letters have been removed from the word in capitals.

These three letters correctly spell a new word without changing their order.

Write in the three missing letters.

EXAMPLE

We DEED the topic of using phones in school. ......**BAT**......

(The word in capitals is DE<u>BAT</u>ED.)

1. My grandad used his old TYRITER to write his memoir. ....

2. The striker beat the defender and VOLLD the ball into the net. ....

3. Despite the accident, there was little NOTABLE damage to the bike. ....

4. Those FLING lights kept me awake all night. ....

5. A MANE is a large, aquatic mammal sometimes called a sea cow. ....

6. Today's temperature will drop due to the SHERLY wind. ....

7. Our whole NERK has been affected by the cyber-attack. ....

8. After playtime, we are watching the INTS sing a song. ....

9. Joe started the race too quickly and IGUE soon set in. ....

10. The bus skidded and COLED with a shopping trolley. ....

Score: .... / 10

Number Sequences

Test 55

You have 6 minutes to complete this test.
You have 10 questions to complete within the time given.

For each question, write in the number that completes the sequence.

EXAMPLE

51   49   47   45   43   ......**41**......   (the sequence is −2)

1) 128 64 32 16 8 ....

2) 47 38 29 20 11 ....

3) 30 27 33 24 36 ....

4) 49 64 81 100 121 ....

5) 301 302 304 307 311 ....

6) 21 42 63 84 105 ....

7) 100 60 40 20 20 ....

8) 99 195 98 205 97 ....

9) 2 5 11 23 47 ....

10) 50 48 44 38 30 ....

Score: .... / 10

Related Numbers

Test 56

You have 6 minutes to complete this test.
You have 10 questions to complete within the time given.

In each question, the three numbers in each group are related in some way.

Write in the number that correctly completes the last group.

EXAMPLE

(5 [9] 13)   (23 [28] 33)   (12 [14] 16)

(The middle number is halfway between the outer two numbers.)

1. (8 [28] 10)   (9 [30] 11)   (3 [......] 7)

2. (3 [17] 8)   (2 [16] 12)   (5 [......] 4)

3. (6 [9] 3)   (7 [28] 8)   (9 [......] 4)

4. (10 [25] 5)   (12 [32] 8)   (14 [......] 6)

5. (6 [10] 4)   (24 [12] 6)   (5 [......] 3)

6. (72 [6] 8)   (27 [0] 9)   (42 [......] 7)

7. (9 [31] 20)   (11 [19] 15)   (15 [......] 25)

8. (3 [47] 20)   (5 [135] 10)   (4 [......] 6)

9. (2 [44] 11)   (6 [132] 11)   (4 [......] 11)

10. (14 [5] 70)   (13 [6] 78)   (15 [......] 105)

Score: .... / 10

Test 57: Word Construction

You have 6 minutes to complete this test.
You have 10 questions to complete within the time given.

In each question, the three words on the second line should go together in the same way as the three words on the first line.

Write in the missing word on the second line.

EXAMPLE

(slap   [last]   this)
(skin   [**kind**]   down)

(word one letter 2, word one letter 3, word two letter 4, word two letter 1)

---

1. (fold   [lock]   back)
(wife   [**fist**]   mist)

2. (main   [nine]   near)
(zips   [**spun**]   undo)

3. (whip   [head]   made)
(scud   [**coal**]   halo)

4. (slip   [link]   khan)
(apex   [**perm**]   moor)

5. (male   [lead]   gold)
(lied   [**edit**]   last)

6. (tofu   [buoy]   bays)
(taxi   [**dial**]   dole)

7. (else   [twee]   with)
(ever   [**user**]   soul)

8. (idol   [lobe]   bile)
(leaf   [**fawn**]   warn)

9. (soda   [goad]   gang)
(visa   [**bias**]   glib)

10. (term   [tome]   into)
(blue   [**peel**]   rope)

Score: .... / 10

Word Combinations

Test 58

You have 6 minutes to complete this test.

You have 10 questions to complete within the time given.

In each question, combine one word from the first group with one word from the second group to create one new word.

The word from the first group always comes first.

Underline the correct word from each group and write in the new word.

EXAMPLE

(<u>tooth</u>   bed   ache)

(skin   sun   <u>pick</u>)   ....toothpick..........

1. (hotel   restaurant   home)
   (food   made   reception)   ....

2. (new   sugar   flour)
   (dust   floss   coat)   ....

3. (rein   pony   ride)
   (tail   rule   horse)   ....

4. (straight   bend   ahead)
   (lean   down   forward)   ....

5. (path   sharp   way)
   (point   beyond   indicate)   ....

6. (sheet   fill   grid)
   (in   open   lock)   ....

7. (ice   water   back)
   (wood   front   cube)   ....

8. (draw   colour   hard)
   (tower   pencil   bridge)   ....

9. (through   give   over)
   (pass   donate   along)   ....

10. (work   car   commute)
    (journey   train   pool)   ....

Score: .... / 10

Test 59 — Antonyms

You have 6 minutes to complete this test.
You have 10 questions to complete within the time given.

In each question, underline the two words (one from each group) that are most opposite in meaning.

EXAMPLE

(acidic   <u>sharp</u>   keen)
(crisp   clever   <u>blunt</u>)

1. (warm   calm   cloudy)
   (snow   unfriendly   hot)

2. (future   memory   present)
   (absent   gift   brain)

3. (fact   express   argue)
   (fluent   slow   speak)

4. (transparent   clear   pour)
   (empty   definite   vague)

5. (cat   rise   duck)
   (stand   goose   bark)

6. (alert   careless   signal)
   (noise   siren   inattentive)

7. (last   first   end)
   (persevere   second   final)

8. (author   novel   book)
   (new   old   poem)

9. (square   less   prime)
   (hexagon   inferior   number)

10. (find   arrest   know)
    (suspect   criminal   clue)

Score: .... / 10

Test 60 — Problem Solving

You have 8 minutes to complete this test.

You have 8 questions to complete within the time given.

In each question, read the information provided and then write in your answer.

EXAMPLE

The classroom clock shows a time of 9:35 am.
The clock is running 6 minutes fast. Break is at 10:15 am.
How long is it in minutes until break starts? ....**46 minutes**....

1. 12 cones are evenly spaced in a straight line across a field. The distance from the 2nd cone to the 5th cone is 15 m.

   How far is it from the 5th cone to the 12th cone? ....

2. A digital clock in a car is incorrectly showing 09:29. The time is quarter past six in the morning.

   How many minutes fast is the car clock running? ....

3. In a year group of 89 children, 43 are learning French only, 32 are learning Spanish only and 7 children are learning both languages.

   How many children are learning neither language? ....

4. In a bag, there are some cubes and triangular prisms. There are no other shapes. There are twice as many cubes as triangular prisms. The shapes have a total of 51 faces.

   How many of each shape are in the bag? ....

5 The library is north of the park.
The supermarket is south of the library.
The cottage is west of the park and north-west of the supermarket.

What direction is it from the library to the cottage?

6 The sum of half of what Lucy's age was two years ago and double what it will be in two years' time is 23.

How old is Lucy?

7 Lisbon is 2 degrees warmer than Rome but 2 degrees colder than Naples.
Rome is 5 degrees warmer than Barcelona but 4 degrees colder than Athens.
Athens and Naples are 18°C.
The temperature in Madrid is the same as in Barcelona.

What is the temperature in Madrid?

8 Josh, Anika, Benji, Wei and Nikoli attend sports clubs after school.
Josh and Wei go to badminton.
Everyone goes to football except Josh.
Anika and Nikoli go to street dance.
Benji goes to rugby and tennis.
Anika wants to go to tennis but doesn't have time.
Josh goes to hockey.

Who goes to the most clubs?

Score: .... / 8

Notes

Answers

Test 1 Move a Letter

- **Q1** i (the new words are **gong** and **bas**i**s**)
- **Q2** u (the new words are **hose** and **mo**u**th**)
- **Q3** t (the new words are **race** and **plan**t)
- **Q4** l (the new words are **word** and **p**l**ace**)
- **Q5** v (the new words are **shoe** and **cur**v**e**)
- **Q6** b (the new words are **tale** and **b**road)
- **Q7** a (the new words are **chin** and **co**a**st**)
- **Q8** g (the new words are **ride** and **clan**g)
- **Q9** e (the new words are **step** and **s**e**ize**)
- **Q10** w (the new words are **sift** and **w**oven)

Test 2 Code Pairs

- **Q1** DYQTF (+3, −3, +2, −2, +1)
- **Q2** UFEWIL (+2, +3, +4, +5, +6, +7)
- **Q3** WEIGH (the code for PUPIL is −1, −4, +2, +2, −6. So, to find the word from VAKIB, reverse the code to +1, +4, −2, −2, +6)
- **Q4** TREMOR (the code for UPLOAD is +4, −5, −3, +8, +4, +2. So, to find the word from XMBUST, reverse the code to −4, +5, +3, −8, −4, −2)
- **Q5** FLOURISH (the code for NOTEBOOK is −2, +2, 0, +6, 0, +5, −5, +3. So, to find the word from DNOARNNK, reverse the code to +2, −2, 0, −6, 0, −5, +5, −3)
- **Q6** SUOIRES (everything reversed)
- **Q7** GUILT (the code for CANOE is −2, −4, −6, −8, −10. So, to find the word from EQCDJ, reverse the code to +2, +4, +6, +8, +10)
- **Q8** WCNEYLUD (+7, −2, −4, +2, −6, +3, −1, −1)
- **Q9** SAJHWNF (+4, −2, +5, +7, +9, +5, +3)
- **Q10** NUCLEAR (the code for DIVIDED is +3, −4, +4, −8, +5, +10, +7. So, to find the word from QQGDJKY, reverse the code to −3, +4, −4, +8, −5, −10, −7)

Test 3 Complete the Sum

- **Q1** 4
- **Q2** 5
- **Q3** 3
- **Q4** 10
- **Q5** 8
- **Q6** 54
- **Q7** 2
- **Q8** 7
- **Q9** 25
- **Q10** 9

Test 4 Missing Three-letter Words

- **Q1** SHE (the word in capitals is **CASHEWS**)
- **Q2** CAN (the word in capitals is **VACANCIES**)
- **Q3** OUR (the word in capitals is **COURAGE**)
- **Q4** GET (the word in capitals is **TOGETHER**)
- **Q5** HAT (the word in capitals is **SHATTERED**)
- **Q6** AIM (the word in capitals is **CLAIMED**)
- **Q7** ALL (the word in capitals is **WALLET**)
- **Q8** NEW (the word in capitals is **RENEWED**)
- **Q9** URN (the word in capitals is **FURNITURE**)
- **Q10** ONE (the word in capitals is **COLONEL**)

Test 5 Code Sets

- **Q1** 1343
- **Q2** ERAS
- **Q3** 5263
- **Q4** 3978
- **Q5** MOLT
- **Q6** 8724
- **Q7** 2416
- **Q8** SLOW
- **Q9** 1643

Test 6 Word Analogies

- **Q1** dig, illuminate (the words describe a functional relationship (used for))
- **Q2** human, rodent (the words describe a relationship to do with parts of the body (have))
- **Q3** train, plane (the words describe a functional relationship (do))

Test 6 answers continue on next page

- **Q4** <u>ferret</u>, <u>eel</u> (the words are adult names for the animals)
- **Q5** <u>won</u>, <u>ate</u> (the words are homophones)
- **Q6** <u>elementary</u>, <u>irate</u> (the words are synonyms)
- **Q7** <u>ward</u>, <u>drawer</u> (the letters in the words are reversed)
- **Q8** <u>never</u>, <u>often</u> (the words are antonyms of adverbs of frequency)
- **Q9** <u>remote</u>, <u>mouse</u> (the words describe a functional relationship (control))
- **Q10** <u>tiny</u>, <u>droll</u> (the words are synonyms)

Test 7 Letters for Numbers

- **Q1** C
- **Q2** B
- **Q3** E
- **Q4** A
- **Q5** A
- **Q6** D
- **Q7** B
- **Q8** E
- **Q9** A
- **Q10** C

Test 8 Related Words

- **Q1** <u>hand</u>, <u>brick</u> (all the others are imperial units of measurement)
- **Q2** <u>rush</u>, <u>soldier</u> (all the others are collective nouns for animals)
- **Q3** <u>hinder</u>, <u>drop</u> (all the others are synonyms for lift)
- **Q4** <u>jigsaw</u>, <u>console</u> (all the others are related to playing board games)
- **Q5** <u>light</u>, <u>festival</u> (all the others are synonyms of unfair)
- **Q6** <u>helicopter</u>, <u>rhombus</u> (all the others are types of bird)
- **Q7** <u>licence</u>, <u>field</u> (all the others are related to travelling by aeroplane)
- **Q8** <u>sugar</u>, <u>yoghurt</u> (all the others are types of knife)
- **Q9** <u>proud</u>, <u>selfish</u> (all the others are synonyms for feeling sorry)
- **Q10** <u>satisfied</u>, <u>distribute</u> (all the others are related to social media)

Test 9 Complete the Third Pair the Same Way

- **Q1** yodel (replace the 1st letter with 'y')
- **Q2** tote (number code 3257)
- **Q3** kin (replace the 1st letter with the last letter)
- **Q4** well (change the 2nd letter from 'a' to 'e')
- **Q5** era (reverse the last three letters)
- **Q6** item (number code 3452)
- **Q7** born (move the 1st letter one letter back in the alphabet)
- **Q8** wilt (replace the last letter with 't')
- **Q9** tan (number code 623)
- **Q10** shoes (change the 'ow' to 'oe')

Test 10 Hidden Words

- **Q1** knew (qui<u>ck new</u>comer)
- **Q2** rate (<u>rat e</u>scaped)
- **Q3** able (keb<u>ab lef</u>tovers)
- **Q4** some (cal<u>ypso me</u>lody)
- **Q5** pier (<u>pie r</u>esting)
- **Q6** ally (<u>all y</u>our)
- **Q7** axis (<u>a</u>nthr<u>ax is</u>)
- **Q8** menu (fisher<u>men u</u>ncovered)
- **Q9** dare (ruine<u>d are</u>na)
- **Q10** type (ci<u>ty per</u>suaded)

Test 11 Letter Connections

- **Q1** r (the four words are your, road, moor and raid)
- **Q2** m (the four words are them, mob, spam and mask)
- **Q3** p (the four words are harp, pray, yelp and page)
- **Q4** k (the four words are plank, knit, steak and kin)
- **Q5** o (the four words are hero, olive, tempo and open)
- **Q6** h (the four words are ash, hedge, high and hill)
- **Q7** e (the four words are theme, elite, quite and every)
- **Q8** d (the four words are amid, drier, fund and draft)

Test 11 answers continue on next page

| Q9 | a (the four words are via, atom, cocoa and again) |
| Q10 | c (the four words are bloc, call, chic and could) |

Test 12 Letter Analogies

Q1	VY (1st letter +2; 2nd letter +4)
Q2	NI (1st letter –5; 2nd letter –8)
Q3	AT (1st letter +3; 2nd letter –3)
Q4	EV (1st letter –10; 2nd letter –2)
Q5	XN (1st letter +6; 2nd letter +9)
Q6	BK (1st letter +5; 2nd letter –1)
Q7	WH (1st letter +11; 2nd letter +2)
Q8	AA (1st letter –6; 2nd letter +3)
Q9	YJ (1st letter –4; 2nd letter 0)
Q10	LN (1st letter +7; 2nd letter +7)

Test 13 Code Sequences

Q1	JT (1st letter: –2; 2nd letter: +3)
Q2	QF (1st letter: +1, +2, +3, +4, +5; 2nd letter: –4)
Q3	ZZ (1st letter: 0, +1, 0, +1, 0; 2nd letter: –2, –4, –6, –8, –10)
Q4	UO (1st letter: –7, +6, –7, +6, –7; 2nd letter: +2, +1, +2, +1, +2)
Q5	GH (1st letter: –5, –4, –3, –2, –1; 2nd letter: every other letter +2)
Q6	KT (1st letter: +2; 2nd letter: +1, +2, +1, +2, +1)
Q7	XW (1st letter: every other letter –1; 2nd letter: +4)
Q8	SX (1st letter: –3; 2nd letter: –2)
Q9	TL (1st letter: every other letter +3; 2nd letter: every other letter –2)
Q10	DX (1st letter: +1; 2nd letter: –1)

Test 14 Missing Three-letter Words

Q1	TOW (the word in capitals is **STOWAWAY**)
Q2	YEW (the word in capitals is **EYEWITNESS**)
Q3	EAT (the word in capitals is **RETREAT**)
Q4	BAR (the word in capitals is **EMBARRASS**)
Q5	HEM (the word in capitals is **ANTHEM**)
Q6	CAN (the word in capitals is **CANKEROUS**)
Q7	OPT (the word in capitals is **ADOPTED**)
Q8	LAY (the word in capitals is **MISLAYS**)
Q9	FOR (the word in capitals is **DEFORMED**)
Q10	ANY (the word in capitals is **MAHOGANY**)

Test 15 Number Sequences

Q1	76 (the sequence is +14)
Q2	3 (the sequence is ÷3)
Q3	68 (the sequence is +2, +4, +8, +16, +32)
Q4	16 (the sequence is decreasing square numbers)
Q5	10 (the sequence is every other one +5 and –5)
Q6	3 (the sequence is 0, –1, –2, –3, –4)
Q7	17 (the sequence is ascending prime numbers)
Q8	480 (the sequence is doubling)
Q9	21 (the sequence is the Fibonacci sequence: each number is the sum of the two preceding numbers)
Q10	20 (the sequence is –11)

Test 16 Related Numbers

a = the first number within the group of three
b = the third number within the group of three

Q1	$37 = (b - a) = (60 - 23)$
Q2	$23 = (a + b) + 3 = (8 + 12) + 3$
Q3	$18 = (a + b^2) = 2 + 4^2$
Q4	$29 = a + (b \times 2) = 9 + (10 \times 2)$
Q5	$11 = (a \div b) + 1 = (30 \div 3) + 1$
Q6	$15 = (a^3 + b) \div 2 = (3^3 + 3) \div 2$
Q7	$9 = (a - b)^2 = (12 - 9)^2$
Q8	$220 = 2(a \times b) = 2 \times (10 \times 11)$
Q9	$2 = (b \div a) - 3 = (15 \div 3) - 3$
Q10	$14 = (2a - b) = (2 \times 11) - 8$

Test 17 Double Meanings

| Q1 | drop |
| | When used as a verb, drop is a synonym of release and reduce. When used as a noun, drop is a synonym of bead and globule. |

Test 17 answers continue on next page

Q2 right

When used as an adjective, right is a synonym of honourable and correct. When used as a noun, right is a synonym of privilege and entitlement.

Q3 stop

When used as a verb, stop is a synonym of prevent and thwart. When used as a noun, stop is a synonym of a station or halt on a bus route or railway.

Q4 bark

When used as a noun, one sense of bark is something that grows on a tree, as are fruit and leaf. In another sense, bark is a type of noise that an animal makes, as are cluck and purr.

Q5 lead

When used as a verb, lead is a synonym of guide and command. When used as a noun, lead is a type of metal, as are copper and aluminium.

Q6 spring

When used as a verb, spring is a synonym of vault and bound. When used as a noun, one sense of spring is as a season, as are winter and summer.

Q7 bolt

When used as a verb, one sense of bolt is a synonym of flee and run. In another sense, bolt is a synonym of fasten and secure.

Q8 trip

When used as a verb, trip is a synonym of fall and stumble. When used as a noun, trip is a synonym of journey and excursion.

Q9 bear

When used as a noun, bear is a type of mammal, as are whale and human. When used as a verb, bear is a synonym of tolerate and endure.

Q10 plague

When used as a verb, plague is a synonym of afflict and trouble. When used as a noun, plague is a synonym of pestilence and epidemic.

Test 18 Word Construction

Q1 left (word two letter 1, word one letter 1, word two letter 3, word two letter 4)

Q2 pine (word one letter 1, word two letter 2, word two letter 1, word one letter 2)

Q3 torn (word one letter 4, word two letter 4, word one letter 2, word two letter 1)

Q4 lied (word one letter 3, word two letter 3, word two letter 2, word one letter 4)

Q5 arid (word one letter 2, word one letter 1, word two letter 2, word two letter 1)

Q6 read (word one letter 1, word one letter 2, word two letter 4, word two letter 1)

Q7 than (word one letter 3, word one letter 4, word two letter 3, word two letter 4)

Q8 nose (word two letter 4, word one letter 2, word two letter 1, word two letter 3)

Q9 noun (word one letter 4, word one letter 3, word two letter 2, word two letter 4)

Q10 riot (word one letter 2, word one letter 3, word two letter 1, word two letter 3)

Test 19 Synonyms

Q1 racket, bat
Q2 edge, border
Q3 signal, indicate
Q4 sharp, keen
Q5 watch, clock
Q6 light, flimsy
Q7 clear, obvious
Q8 hold, accommodate
Q9 total, utter
Q10 right, privilege

Test 20 Problem Solving

Q1 4

Aisha likes apples, grapes, oranges, mangoes and strawberries (5). Jasmine only likes mangoes (1). Aisha likes 4 more fruits than Jasmine.

Q2 25p

Jeans in Shop A are £25 − 25% = £18.75. Adding a £5 delivery change makes a total of £23.75.
Jeans in Shop B are £29 − 50% = £14.50. Adding a £9 delivery change makes a total of £23.50.
Therefore, £23.75 − £23.50 = £0.25 or 25p.

Test 20 answers continue on next page

Q3 **307 litres**

Pool C contains 400 + 50 = 450 litres.
Pool E loses 12 litres per day. After a week (7 days), it contains: 350 − 84 = 266 litres.
Pool B contains 266 + 20 = 286 litres.
Pool D contains half as much as Pool B, which is 286 ÷ 2 = 143 litres.
Therefore, Pool C − Pool D = 450 − 143 = 307 litres.

Q4 **9:26 pm**

Subtract 45 minutes from 10:41 am to find the current time, which is 9:56 am. Subtract 12 hours, which makes it 9:56 pm, the previous night. Subtract another 30 minutes, which means the time was 9:26 pm.

Q5 **68**

$5^2 + 2^2 = 25 + 4 = 29$
$7^2 + 8^2 = 49 + 64 = 113$
The smallest square number is 4. The largest square number is 64, so 4 + 64 = 68.

Q6 **great uncle**

Because Samuel is Evan's brother, Violet is also Samuel's grandmother. Violet's brother-in-law is William, which means William is the brother of Violet's spouse (i.e. Samuel's grandfather).
If William is the brother of Samuel's grandfather, then William is Samuel's great uncle.

Q7 **2nd**

Runner A falls back to 3rd place. Runner B moves forward to 4th place. At the finish, Runner B overtakes Runner A, meaning Runner B finishes 3rd immediately behind Runner C, who comes 2nd.

Q8 **west**

Sanjay starts in a southerly direction. After turning left, he walks east. After turning right, he walks south again. After turning right again, he is facing west to admire the view.

Test 21 Move a Letter

Q1 k (the new words are **sill** and **thank**)
Q2 b (the new words are **lame** and **bring**)
Q3 o (the new words are **pint** and **avoid**)
Q4 g (the new words are **bean** and **grace**)
Q5 a (the new words are **rise** and **along**)
Q6 f (the new words are **lies** and **rifle**)

Q7 l (the new words are **seep** and **least**)
Q8 r (the new words are **band** and **heart**)
Q9 e (the new words are **very** and **prime**)
Q10 u (the new words are **debt** and **suite**)

Test 22 Code Pairs

Q1 JPUU (+2, +1, +2, +1)
Q2 DIWHN (−1, −3, −5, −7, −9)
Q3 PURSUE (the code for FAMILY is 0, +1, 0, +2, 0, +3. So, to find the word from PVRUUH, reverse the code to 0, −1, 0, −2, 0, −3)
Q4 LGSOCK (+6, −5, +4, −3, +2, −1)
Q5 KERB (the code for COLD is +3, +1, +2, +1. So, to find the word from NFTC, reverse the code to −3, −1, −2, −1)
Q6 LWDWP (+10, +5, +9, +4, +8)
Q7 KINGDOM (the code for HUNDRED is all letters +2. So, to find the word from MKPIFQO, reverse the code to all letters −2)
Q8 SMILE (the code for JAUNT is −5, +3, −7, +3, −6. So, to find the word from NPBOY, reverse the code to +5, −3, +7, −3, +6)
Q9 FEILER (everything is reversed)
Q10 WALTZ (the code for EXACT is −1, +2, −3, +4, −5. So, to find the word from VCIXU, reverse the code to +1, −2, +3, −4, +5)

Test 23 Complete the Sum

Q1 9
Q2 12
Q3 40
Q4 61
Q5 7
Q6 9
Q7 54
Q8 198
Q9 8
Q10 4

Test 24 Missing Three-letter Words

Q1 EVE (the word in capitals is **REVEALING**)
Q2 OIL (the word in capitals is **BOILING**)

Test 24 answers continue on next page

Q3	TEA (the word in capitals is **STEALTHY**)	Q3	D	
Q4	USE (the word in capitals is **TROUSERS**)	Q4	E	
Q5	OWL (the word in capitals is **NARROWLY**)	Q5	E	
Q6	EAR (the word in capitals is **REHEARSE**)	Q6	A	
Q7	APE (the word in capitals is **CHEAPER**)	Q7	B	
Q8	ORE (the word in capitals is **FORENSIC**)	Q8	D	
Q9	FIN (the word in capitals is **REFINERY**)	Q9	A	
Q10	ILL (the word in capitals is **VILLAIN**)	Q10	E	

Test 25 Code Sets

Q1 1524
Q2 STOP
Q3 1625
Q4 6053
Q5 FIND
Q6 6270
Q7 5314
Q8 RUSH
Q9 2145

Test 26 Word Analogies

Q1 bury, write (the words are homophones)
Q2 cast, catch (the words are synonyms)
Q3 yacht, canoe (the words describe a functional relationship (moves))
Q4 slowly, softly (the words are adverb antonyms)
Q5 armpit, passport (the words are compound nouns)
Q6 type, measure (the words describe a functional relationship (used to))
Q7 spam, emit (the letters in the words are reversed)
Q8 foot, neck (the words describe a relationship between clothing and body parts)
Q9 punch, glue (the words describe a functional relationship (is made using))
Q10 cow, sow (the words are the names for the female animals)

Test 27 Letters for Numbers

Q1 C
Q2 B

Test 28 Related Words

Q1 axle, wing (all the other words are parts of a ship)
Q2 table, picnic (all the other words are synonyms for stopping someone from doing something)
Q3 goat, adult (all the other words are synonyms for making jokes)
Q4 river, professor (all the other words are palindromes that read the same forwards and backwards)
Q5 ancient, rattle (all the other words are types of dance)
Q6 engine, desert (all the other words are states of matter of water)
Q7 hamster, wolf (all the other words are animal names that can be singular or plural)
Q8 emit, watch (all the other words are synonyms for forgetting to do something)
Q9 courage, lack (all the other words can be preceded by the suffix re-)
Q10 continent, region (all the other words are types of human settlement)

Test 29 Complete the Third Pair the Same Way

Q1 liar (reverse the letters)
Q2 worship (change the 'a' to an 'o')
Q3 severe (replace the first letter with 's')
Q4 diet (code 1324)
Q5 gauge (change the 'or' to 'au')
Q6 angle (reverse the last two letters)
Q7 fund (code 1534)
Q8 verse (swap the positions of the 1st and 4th letters)

Test 29 answers continue on next page

Q9 lens (code 6234)
Q10 chest (the 3rd letter becomes the next vowel in the alphabet, the 4th letter becomes the next consonant in the alphabet)

Test 30 Hidden Words

Q1 ship (su**shi p**latter)
Q2 also (**to**tal s**o**lution)
Q3 gnat (stun**n**ing **nat**ural)
Q4 edge (stu**d**i**ed ge**ography)
Q5 both (ro**bot h**ome)
Q6 undo (westbo**und on**)
Q7 exam (compl**ex am**phibious)
Q8 bias (ti**bia s**lipping)
Q9 wind (**new ind**ependent)
Q10 knot (thi**ck not**epad)

Test 31 Letter Connections

Q1 b (the four words are blurb, bid, plumb and bred)
Q2 w (the four words are renew, won, brow and when)
Q3 e (the four words are lease, edit, huge and eager)
Q4 s (the four words are opus, slot, alias and show)
Q5 f (the four words are waif, flung, clef and flora)
Q6 g (the four words are stung, gash, rang and glow)
Q7 i (the four words are sari, ideal, umami and iota)
Q8 l (the four words are renal, lit, bowl and leach)
Q9 n (the four words are haven, nous, login and node)
Q10 t (the four words are feet, tsar, merit and town)

Test 32 Letter Analogies

Q1 PU (1st letter: +2; 2nd letter: +3)
Q2 HS (1st letter: +1; 2nd letter: –5)
Q3 OR (1st letter: –2; 2nd letter: –1)
Q4 NV (1st letter: –4; 2nd letter: +4)
Q5 WE (1st letter: +8; 2nd letter: –2)
Q6 AK (1st letter: –3; 2nd letter: +6)
Q7 GS (1st letter: –5; 2nd letter: –4)
Q8 TQ (1st letter: –6; 2nd letter: +9)
Q9 CZ (1st letter: +3; 2nd letter: 0)
Q10 SB (1st letter: +1; 2nd letter: –10)

Test 33 Code Sequences

Q1 UI (1st letter: +2, +3, +4, +5, +6; 2nd letter: –3)
Q2 MP (1st letter: +4; 2nd letter: –2)
Q3 PA (1st letter: every other letter +1; 2nd letter: –2, –3, –2, –3, –2)
Q4 GG (1st letter: –1, –2, –3, –4, –5; 2nd letter: 0, +2, 0, +2, 0)
Q5 WL (1st letter: –1; 2nd letter: +3)
Q6 LJ (1st letter: –4; 2nd letter: –5, –4, –3, –2, –1)
Q7 CN (1st letter: +3, +1, +3, +1, +3; 2nd letter: +2)
Q8 WB (1st letter: +1, +2, +1, +2, +1; 2nd letter: every other letter –1)
Q9 TV (1st letter: every other letter +2; 2nd letter: –1)
Q10 BA (1st letter: +1, +3, +5, +7, +9; 2nd letter: –1, –3, –5, –7, –9)

Test 34 Missing Three-letter Words

Q1 FIR (the word in capitals is **MISFIRING**)
Q2 HER (the word in capitals is **FEATHERED**)
Q3 YOU (the word in capitals is **PAYOUT**)
Q4 AWE (the word in capitals is **SEAWEED**)
Q5 HAS (the word in capitals is **PURCHASE**)
Q6 CUT (the word in capitals is **ACUTE**)
Q7 DIE (the word in capitals in **GRADIENT**)
Q8 GUM (the word in capitals is **LEGUMES**)
Q9 POD (the word in capitals is **HYPODERMIC**)
Q10 EBB (the word in capitals is **PEBBLES**)

Test 35 Number Sequences

Q1 10 (the sequence is –9)
Q2 243 (the sequence is tripling each number)

Test 35 answers continue on next page

Q3 39 (the sequence is adding consecutive odd numbers, +1, +3, +5, +7, +9)

Q4 1 (the sequence is decreasing cube numbers)

Q5 6 (the sequence is halving each number)

Q6 13 (the sequence is every other one −2 and +2)

Q7 32 (the sequence is each number is the product (×) of the two preceding numbers)

Q8 15 (the sequence is every other one +10 and −5)

Q9 129 (the sequence is adding consecutive even numbers, +2, +4, +6, +8, +10)

Q10 11 (the sequence is descending prime numbers)

Test 36 Related Numbers

a = the first number within the group of three
b = the third number within the group of three

Q1 $7 = b \div a = (21 \div 3)$

Q2 $28 = a + b = (16 + 12)$

Q3 $16 = (a^2 - b) = (6^2 - 20)$

Q4 $100 = 2(b - a) = 2 \times (75 - 25)$

Q5 $66 = (a + b^3) = (2 + 4^3)$

Q6 $6 = (a - b) \div 2 = (28 - 16) \div 2$

Q7 $49 = (a \times b) - 5 = (6 \times 9) - 5$

Q8 $52 = (a^2 + b) + 2 = (7^2 + 1) + 2$

Q9 $32 = a + 2b = 8 + (2 \times 12)$

Q10 $12 = 3(a \times b) = 3 \times (1 \times 4)$

Test 37 Double Meanings

Q1 watch
When used as a verb, watch is a synonym of observe and view. When used as a noun, watch is a type of device for telling the time, as are sundial and clock.

Q2 make
When used as a noun, make is a synonym of brand and marque. When used as a verb, make is a synonym of assemble and build.

Q3 address
When used as a noun, one sense of address means a spoken presentation, as do speech and lecture. In another sense, address means a specific place, as do whereabouts and location.

Q4 flush
When used as an adjective, flush is a synonym of flat and level. When used as a verb, flush is a synonym of inundate and wash.

Q5 wrong
When used as an adjective, wrong is a synonym of mistaken and incorrect. When used as a noun, wrong is a synonym of injustice and violation.

Q6 prompt
When used as a verb, prompt is a synonym of cause and encourage. When used as an adverb, prompt is a synonym of exactly and sharp.

Q7 express
When used as an adjective, express is a synonym of rapid and speedy. When used as a verb, express is a synonym of articulate and convey.

Q8 clear
When used as a verb, clear is a synonym of empty and unblock. When used as an adjective, clear is a synonym of obvious and evident.

Q9 skate
When used as a verb, skate is a synonym of slide and glide. When used as a noun, one sense of skate is a type of flat fish, as are flounder and plaice.

Q10 complete
When used as an adjective, complete is a synonym of absolute and total. When used as a verb, complete is a synonym of conclude and finish.

Test 38 Word Combinations

Q1 airtight (air and tight)

Q2 quicksilver (quick and silver)

Q3 flowchart (flow and chart)

Q4 proofread (proof and read)

Q5 undertake (under and take)

Q6 knighthood (knight and hood)

Q7 yearbook (year and book)

Q8 loudspeaker (loud and speaker)

Q9 jumpsuit (jump and suit)

Q10 breakfast (break and fast)

Test 39 Synonyms

- **Q1** yak, prattle
- **Q2** book, reserve
- **Q3** file, folder
- **Q4** field, pitch
- **Q5** row, argument
- **Q6** star, celebrity
- **Q7** twist, wind
- **Q8** address, lecture
- **Q9** dessert, sweet
- **Q10** clip, prune

Test 40 Antonyms

- **Q1** close, far
- **Q2** future, past
- **Q3** grave, trivial
- **Q4** mint, damaged
- **Q5** reject, grant
- **Q6** rest, toil
- **Q7** calculated, unplanned
- **Q8** harmful, innocuous
- **Q9** hunch, proof
- **Q10** tomorrow, yesterday

Test 41 Move a Letter

- **Q1** n (the new words are **moth** and **dozen**)
- **Q2** d (the new words are **tire** and **crowd**)
- **Q3** c (the new words are **rash** and **cover**)
- **Q4** m (the new words are **oral** and **realm**)
- **Q5** k (the new words are **flan** and **think**)
- **Q6** i (the new words are **bran** and **image**)
- **Q7** v (the new words are **care** and **seven**)
- **Q8** p (the new words are **robe** and **clamp**)
- **Q9** b (the new words are **reel** and **fibre**)
- **Q10** h (the new words are **later** and **shock**)

Test 42 Code Pairs

- **Q1** DJLR (+1, +2, +3, +4)
- **Q2** IMPLY (the code for ORGAN is −1, 0, −2, 0, −1. So, to find the word from HMNLX, reverse the code to +1, 0, +2, 0, +1)
- **Q3** UPGRADE (the letters are reversed)
- **Q4** LNLC (+2, −1, +1, −2)
- **Q5** CWZPLN (−3, −4, −3, −4, −3, −4)
- **Q6** REASON (the code for MOTHER is +5, +5, +4, +4, +3, +3. So, to find the word from WJEWRQ, reverse the code to −5, −5, −4, −4, −3, −3)
- **Q7** ONYX (the code for ZEAL is +1, −2, +3, −4. So, to find the word from PLBT, reverse the code to −1, +2, −3, +4)
- **Q8** IHLJW (+7, +3, +5, +1, +9)
- **Q9** STOMACH (the code for CHARITY is +2, +3, +2, +3, +2, +3, +2. So, to find the word from UWQPCFJ, reverse the code to −2, −3, −2, −3, −2, −3, −2)
- **Q10** IAWJ (−2, −4, +11, −6)

Test 43 Complete the Sum

- **Q1** 30
- **Q2** 16
- **Q3** 56
- **Q4** 10
- **Q5** 2
- **Q6** 9
- **Q7** 3
- **Q8** 50
- **Q9** 5
- **Q10** 20

Test 44 Missing Three-letter Words

- **Q1** EMU (the word in capitals is **EMULATE**)
- **Q2** FRY (the word in capitals is **BELFRY**)
- **Q3** RUE (the word in capitals is **GRUELLING**)
- **Q4** OWE (the word in capitals is **PROWESS**)
- **Q5** VIA (the word in capitals is **DEVIATE**)
- **Q6** SKI (the word in capitals is **BASKING**)
- **Q7** TOO (the word in capitals is **MISTOOK**)
- **Q8** TIC (the word in capitals is **PESTICIDE**)
- **Q9** JAR (the word in capitals is **JARGON**)
- **Q10** AIR (the word in capitals is **PAIRINGS**)

Test 45 Code Sets

Q1 2584
Q2 IDLE
Q3 9548
Q4 1268
Q5 COME
Q6 8972
Q7 2943
Q8 THAN
Q9 2759

Test 46 Word Analogies

Q1 live, nuts (the letters in the words are reversed)
Q2 cube, tetrahedron (the words are 3D shapes)
Q3 baleful, grave (the words are synonyms)
Q4 east, west (the words describe a relationship (cardinal directions))
Q5 rigid, obtuse (the words are antonyms)
Q6 glean, parsley (the words are anagrams)
Q7 key, latch (the words describe a functional relationship (lock))
Q8 elbow, neck (the words describe how the joints of the body move)
Q9 Zeus, Poseidon (the words are the Roman and Greek equivalent deities)
Q10 justice, courage (the words are abstract nouns)

Test 47 Letters for Numbers

Q1 B
Q2 E
Q3 A
Q4 C
Q5 B
Q6 A
Q7 D
Q8 C
Q9 E
Q10 C

Test 48 Related Words

Q1 crawl, centipede (all the other words are types of insect)
Q2 bat, evening (all the other words are associated with breakfast)
Q3 weather, foreign (all the other words rhyme)
Q4 analyst, dentist (all the other words are people who work with animals)
Q5 correct, fix (all the other words are synonyms for making a mistake)
Q6 moon, year (all the other words are times of day)
Q7 tortoise, crab (all the other words are animals with flippers)
Q8 join, coffin (all the other words are homophones of types of food (berry, meat, cereal))
Q9 cover, trust (all the other words can be preceded by the suffix de-)
Q10 cooking, brush (all the other words are types of paint for art)

Test 49 Complete the Third Pair the Same Way

Q1 bun (remove the 3rd letter)
Q2 foil (change the 'u' to an 'i')
Q3 rat (reverse the middle three letters)
Q4 tear (code 5627)
Q5 gave (code 5123)
Q6 crypto (change the last letter to 'o')
Q7 world (change to 'ea' to 'or')
Q8 also (code 7832)
Q9 peels (reverse the letters)
Q10 ears (remove the 1st letter and add an 's' at the end of the word)

Test 50 Hidden Words

Q1 fort (**for t**he)
Q2 area (ma**rina real**ly)
Q3 stop (fir**st op**ponent)
Q4 tent (bi**tten th**e)
Q5 lean (fragi**le and**)
Q6 raft (weathe**r aft**er)

Test 50 answers continue on next page

Q7 chef (qui**che fe**ll)

Q8 icon (mu**sic on**line)

Q9 putt (in**put t**hat)

Q10 rota (**trot a**long)

Test 51 Letter Connections

Q1 u (the four words are menu, unit, haiku and upend)

Q2 z (the four words are glitz, zone, topaz and zero)

Q3 a (the four words are area, aide, saga and ahead)

Q4 y (the four words are fully, yours, forty and yeast)

Q5 p (the four words are polyp, pie, carp and pace)

Q6 h (the four words are loch, hover, pith and haunt)

Q7 c (the four words are talc, cat, lilac and coup)

Q8 e (the four words are spore, ebony, wine and epic)

Q9 r (the four words are boar, ruddy, deter and radar)

Q10 g (the four words are agog, grub, blog and groom)

Test 52 Letter Analogies

Q1 **TO** (1st letter: +3; 2nd letter: +2)

Q2 **XN** (1st letter: –8; 2nd letter: –4)

Q3 **NC** (1st letter: +5; 2nd letter: –5)

Q4 **IL** (1st letter: +4; 2nd letter: –11)

Q5 **ZB** (1st letter: –7; 2nd letter: +4)

Q6 **GI** (1st letter: +5; 2nd letter: +5)

Q7 **CF** (1st letter: –9; 2nd letter: –6)

Q8 **JJ** (1st letter: +3; 2nd letter: –3)

Q9 **EH** (1st letter: 0; 2nd letter: +10)

Q10 **OK** (1st letter: +9; 2nd letter: +9)

Test 53 Code Sequences

Q1 **LR** (1st letter: +2; 2nd letter: +1)

Q2 **OZ** (1st letter: –2, –1, –2, –1, –2; 2nd letter: +5)

Q3 **DH** (1st letter: 0, +1, +2, +3, +4; 2nd letter: –3)

Q4 **QU** (1st letter: –4; 2nd letter: +1, –2, +3, –4, +5)

Q5 **VF** (1st letter: every other letter +1; 2nd letter: –3, –5, –3, –5, –3)

Q6 **UA** (1st letter: +4, –2, +4, –2, +4; 2nd letter: every other letter –2)

Q7 **JQ** (1st letter: –6; 2nd letter: +6)

Q8 **CT** (1st letter: every other letter +3; 2nd letter: +2, +4, +6, +8, +10)

Q9 **SL** (1st letter: –1, –2, –3, –4, –5; 2nd letter: +3)

Q10 **ZN** (1st letter: +1, +3, +5, +7, +9; 2nd letter: –4, –1, –4, –1, –4)

Test 54 Missing Three-letter Words

Q1 PEW (the word in capitals is **TYPEWRITER**)

Q2 EYE (the word in capitals is **VOLLEYED**)

Q3 ICE (the word in capitals is **NOTICEABLE**)

Q4 ASH (the word in capitals is **FLASHING**)

Q5 ATE (the word in capitals is **MANATEE**)

Q6 OUT (the word in capitals is **SOUTHERLY**)

Q7 TWO (the word in capitals is **NETWORK**)

Q8 FAN (the word in capitals is **INFANTS**)

Q9 FAT (the word in capitals is **FATIGUE**)

Q10 LID (the word in capitals is **COLLIDED**)

Test 55 Number Sequences

Q1 4 (the sequence is halving each number)

Q2 2 (the sequence is –9)

Q3 21 (the sequence is every other one +3 and –3)

Q4 144 (the sequence is increasing square numbers)

Q5 316 (the sequence is +1, +2, +3, +4, +5)

Q6 126 (the sequence is +21)

Q7 0 (the sequence is each number is the difference between the two preceding numbers)

Q8 215 (the sequence is every other one –1 and +10)

Q9 95 (the sequence is doubling and +1)

Q10 20 (the sequence is descending consecutive even numbers, –2, –4, –6, –8, –10)

Test 56 Related Numbers

a = the first number within the group of three
b = the third number within the group of three

Q1 $20 = (a + b) + 10 = (3 + 7) + 10$
Q2 $29 = a^2 + b = 5^2 + 4$
Q3 $18 = (a \times b) \div 2 = (9 \times 4) \div 2$
Q4 $34 = 2a + b = (14 \times 2) + 6$
Q5 $4 = b^2 - a = 3^2 - 5$
Q6 $3 = (a \div b) - 3 = (42 \div 7) - 3$
Q7 $35 = 2b - a = (2 \times 25) - 15$
Q8 $70 = a^3 + b = 4^3 + 6$
Q9 $88 = 2a \times b = (2 \times 4) \times 11$
Q10 $7 = b \div a = 105 \div 15$

Test 57 Word Construction

Q1 **fist** (word one letter 3, word one letter 2, word two letter 3, word two letter 4)
Q2 **spun** (word one letter 4, word one letter 3, word two letter 1, word two letter 2)
Q3 **coal** (word one letter 2, word two letter 4, word two letter 2, word two letter 3)
Q4 **perm** (word one letter 2, word one letter 3, word two letter 4, word two letter 1)
Q5 **edit** (word one letter 3, word one letter 4, word one letter 2, word two letter 4)
Q6 **dial** (word two letter 1, word one letter 4, word one letter 2, word two letter 3)
Q7 **user** (word two letter 3, word two letter 1, word one letter 1, word one letter 4)
Q8 **fawn** (word one letter 4, word one letter 3, word two letter 1, word two letter 4)
Q9 **bias** (word two letter 4, word one letter 2, word one letter 4, word one letter 3)
Q10 **peel** (word two letter 3, word two letter 4, word one letter 4, word one letter 2)

Test 58 Word Combinations

Q1 homemade (<u>home</u> and <u>made</u>)
Q2 sugarcoat (<u>sugar</u> and <u>coat</u>)
Q3 ponytail (<u>pony</u> and <u>tail</u>)
Q4 straightforward (<u>straight</u> and <u>forward</u>)
Q5 waypoint (<u>way</u> and <u>point</u>)
Q6 gridlock (<u>grid</u> and <u>lock</u>)
Q7 waterfront (<u>water</u> and <u>front</u>)
Q8 drawbridge (<u>draw</u> and <u>bridge</u>)
Q9 overpass (<u>over</u> and <u>pass</u>)
Q10 carpool (<u>car</u> and <u>pool</u>)

Test 59 Antonyms

Q1 <u>warm</u>, <u>unfriendly</u>
Q2 <u>present</u>, <u>absent</u>
Q3 <u>express</u>, <u>slow</u>
Q4 <u>clear</u>, <u>vague</u>
Q5 <u>duck</u>, <u>stand</u>
Q6 <u>alert</u>, <u>inattentive</u>
Q7 <u>first</u>, <u>final</u>
Q8 <u>novel</u>, <u>old</u>
Q9 <u>prime</u>, <u>inferior</u>
Q10 <u>know</u>, <u>suspect</u>

Test 60 Problem Solving

Q1 **35 m**

There are three equal gaps between the 2nd cone and the 5th cone, so the gap between each cone is 15 m ÷ 3 = 5 m. There are 7 equal gaps between the 5th cone and the 12th cone, so the total distance between them is 7 × 5 m = 35 m.

Q2 **194 minutes**

Add 45 minutes to 6:15 to complete the hour to 7:00. Add 120 minutes to complete the next two hours to 9:00. Add 29 minutes to reach 9:29. 45 + 120 + 29 = 194.

Q3 **7 children**

43 (French) + 32 (Spanish) + 7 (both) = 82. There are 89 children, so 89 − 82 = 7.

Q4 **6 cubes and 3 triangular prisms**

The number of triangular prisms can be represented by x. A triangular prism has 5 faces, which can be represented by $5x$. There are twice as many cubes as triangular prisms, which can be expressed as $2x$. A cube has 6 faces, which can be represented as $2x \times 6 = 12x$.
Therefore, $12x + 5x = 51$. It follows that $17x = 51$. Divide 51 by 17 to find the value of x (the number of triangular prisms) and double this to find the number of cubes.

Test 60 answers continue on next page

Q5 **south-west**

Three places sit on a north-south line. Because the cottage is north-west of the supermarket and west of the park, the order from north to south must be library, park, supermarket. The cottage must therefore be south-west of the library.

Q6 **8 years old**

Lucy's age (x) two years ago can be represented by $x - 2$. Her age in two years' time can be represented by $x + 2$. Half of her age two years ago can be represented by $\frac{1}{2}(x - 2)$. Double her age in two years' time can be represented by $2(x + 2)$. Therefore:
$\frac{1}{2}(x - 2) + 2(x + 2) = 23$
Double both sides of the equation to cancel out the $\frac{1}{2}$: $(x - 2) + 4(x + 2) = 46$
Multiply out the brackets: $x - 2 + 4x + 8 = 46$
Simplify: $5x + 6 = 46$
Therefore, $5x = 40$ and $x = 8$

Q7 **9°C**

Rome is 4 degrees colder than Athens, therefore, $18 - 4 = 14°C$. Rome is 5 degrees warmer than Barcelona, therefore, $14 - 5 = 9°C$. The temperature in Madrid is the same as in Barcelona. Therefore, Madrid like Barcelona is 9°C.

Q8 **Benji**

Josh goes to badminton and hockey (2);
Anika goes to street dance and football (2);
Benji goes to rugby, tennis and football (3);
Wei goes to badminton and football (2);
Nikoli goes to street dance and football (2).

Notes

ACKNOWLEDGEMENTS

The author and publisher are grateful to the copyright holders for permission to use quoted materials and images.

Every effort has been made to trace copyright holders and obtain their permission for the use of copyright material. The author and publisher will gladly receive information enabling them to rectify any error or omission in subsequent editions. All facts are correct at time of going to press.

Published by Collins
An imprint of HarperCollins*Publishers* Limited
1 London Bridge Street
London SE1 9GF

HarperCollins*Publishers*
Macken House
39/40 Mayor Street Upper
Dublin 1
D01 C9W8
Ireland

ISBN: 978-0-00-876050-2

First published 2025

10 9 8 7 6 5 4 3 2 1

© HarperCollins*Publishers* Limited 2025

All rights reserved. No part of this publication may be reproduced, stored in a retrieval system, or transmitted, in any form or by any means, electronic, mechanical, photocopying, recording or otherwise, without the prior permission of Collins.

Without limiting the exclusive rights of any author, contributor or the publisher of this publication, any unauthorised use of this publication to train generative artificial intelligence (AI) technologies is expressly prohibited. HarperCollins also exercise their rights under Article 4(3) of the Digital Single Market Directive 2019/790 and expressly reserve this publication from the text and data mining exception.

British Library Cataloguing in Publication Data.

A CIP record of this book is available from the British Library.

Author: Giles Clare
Publisher: Clare Souza
Project Manager: Richard Toms
Editorial: Charlotte Christensen
Cover Design: Sarah Duxbury
Text and Page Design: Ian Wrigley
Layout and Artwork: QBS
Production: Bethany Brohm
Printed in the United Kingdom by Martins the Printers

MIX
Paper | Supporting responsible forestry
FSC
www.fsc.org
FSC™ C007454

This book contains FSC™ certified paper and other controlled sources to ensure responsible forest management.

For more information visit: www.harpercollins.co.uk/green